GREAT MYSTERIES

The Bermuda Triangle

OPPOSING VIEWPOINTS®

GREAT MYSTERIES

The Bermuda Triangle

OPPOSING VIEWPOINTS®

Look for these and other exciting *Great Mysteries: Opposing Viewpoints* books:

Alternative Healing

Amelia Earhart

Anastasia, Czarina or Fake?

Animal Communication

Artificial Intelligence

The Assassination of Abraham Lincoln

The Assassination of President Kennedy

Astrology

Atlantis

The Beginning of Language

The Bermuda Triangle

Bigfoot

Custer's Last Stand

The Devil

Dinosaurs

The Discovery of America

El Dorado, Land of Gold

The End of the World

The Fall of the Roman Empire

ESP

Evolution

Haunted Houses

Jack the Ripper

King Arthur

Life After Death

Living in Space

The Loch Ness Monster

The Lost Colony of Roanoke

Miracles

Mysteries of the Moon

Mysteries of Space

Noah's Ark

Pearl Harbor

Poltergeists

President Truman and the Atomic Bomb

Pyramids

Reincarnation

Relativity

Shamans

The Shroud of Turin

The Solar System

Stonehenge

The Trojan War

UFOs

Unicorns

Vampires

Voodoo

Water Monsters

Witches

GREAT MYSTERIES

The Bermuda Triangle

OPPOSING VIEWPOINTS®

by Norma Gaffron

Greenhaven Press, Inc.   P.O. Box 289009, San Diego, California 92198-9009

Library of Congress Cataloging-in-Publication Data

Gaffron, Norma, 1931-
  The Bermuda Triangle : opposing viewpoints / by Norma Gaffron.
    p. cm. — (Great mysteries)
  Includes bibliographical references and index.
  ISBN 1-56510-217-7 (alk. paper)
  1. Bermuda Triangle—Juvenile literature. [1. Bermuda Triangle.]
I. Title. II. Series: Great mysteries (Saint Paul, Minn.)
G558.G33 1995
001.9'4—dc20   94-555
                                        CIP
                                        AC

To Bernie, Mike, Tim, and Patty—for all the good memories of sailing in the Bermuda Triangle.

Contents

	Introduction	9
One	The Bermuda Triangle: Myth or Fact?	10
Two	Out of the Past	20
Three	Nature and Its Tricks	32
Four	More Mysteries, More Explanations	56
Five	Other Times, Other Places	76
Six	The Mystery Remains	92
	For Further Exploration	99
	Works Consulted	103
	Index	107
	About the Author	111
	Picture Credits	112

Introduction

This book is written for the curious—those who want to explore the mysteries that are everywhere. To be human is to be constantly surrounded by wonderment. How do birds fly? Are ghosts real? Can animals and people communicate? Was King Arthur a real person or a myth? Why did Amelia Earhart disappear? Did history really happen the way we think it did? Where did the world come from? Where is it going?

Great Mysteries: Opposing Viewpoints books are intended to offer the reader an opportunity to explore some of the many mysteries that both trouble and intrigue us. For the span of each book, we want the reader to feel that he or she is a scientist investigating the extinction of the dinosaurs, an archaeologist searching for clues to the origin of the great Egyptian pyramids, a psychic detective testing the existence of ESP.

One thing all mysteries have in common is that there is no ready answer. Often there are *many* answers but none on which even the majority of authorities agrees. *Great Mysteries: Opposing Viewpoints* books introduce the intriguing views of the experts, allowing the reader to participate in their explorations, their theories, and their disagreements as they try to explain the mysteries of our world.

But most readers won't want to stop here. These *Great Mysteries: Opposing Viewpoints* aim to stimulate the reader's curiosity. Although truth is often impossible to discover, the search is fascinating. It is up to the reader to examine the evidence, to decide whether the answer is there—or to explore further.

"Penetrating so many secrets, we cease to believe in the unknowable. But there it sits nevertheless, calmly licking its chops."

H.L. Mencken, American essayist

One

The Bermuda Triangle: Myth or Fact?

On December 5, 1945, five U.S. Navy torpedo bombers took off from the Fort Lauderdale, Florida, airport. World War II had been over for three months, so this was to be a routine training exercise. One plane was short its gunner: Cpl. Allan Kosnar had had a strange feeling that he should not go on the flight, and he had asked that someone else go instead. Because he had already completed his required flight time for the month, his request to be excused had been granted. His place was not filled, however. No one knows why.

Flight 19

That left fourteen men—five pilots, five radio operators, and four gunners—on Flight 19. The pilots, who were experienced aviators, were studying advanced navigational methods and low-level bombing techniques. Each aircraft carried enough fuel to enable it to cruise for five and a half hours, even though the projected flight time was just two hours. No one had reason to expect that anything unusual would happen during this mission.

The bombers started taking off at 2 P.M. Ten minutes later all five planes were airborne and flying east over the Atlantic Ocean. When they finished

(Opposite page) Navy Avenger aircraft like those of the legendary Flight 19 fly in formation.

target practice, they began a navigation training drill. The drill was to take them east 160 miles, north 40 miles, then west-southwest back to their base. It was a simple triangular pattern.

At about 3:15 P.M., the radio operator at the Fort Lauderdale Naval Air Station tower received an unusual communication from Lt. C.C. Taylor, pilot of one plane and commander of the four other pilots on the training flight. He reported that his compasses were not reading properly. Charles Berlitz, in his book *The Bermuda Triangle*, says that Taylor then transmitted this radio message: "This is an emergency. We seem to be off course. We cannot see land. . . . Repeat. . . . We cannot see land."

Radio tower operators knew something was terribly wrong when Flight 19 pilot Lt. C.C. Taylor frantically radioed on a clear day, "We seem to be lost."

The tower radioed back, "What is your position?"

Taylor replied, "We are not sure of our position. We cannot be sure just where we are. . . . We seem to be lost. . . ."

When the tower radioed instructions to "assume bearing due west," Taylor said, "We don't know which way is west. Everything is wrong. . . . Strange. . . . We can't be sure of any direction— even the ocean doesn't look as it should. . . ."

The tower operators were puzzled. On this typical south Florida winter day, land should have been clearly visible. The morning had been chilly, but the afternoon was balmy with clear skies. Surface winds of twenty knots (about twenty-three miles per hour), with gusts to thirty (thirty-five miles per hour) would have been rough for small craft, but Flight 19's TBM Avengers were built to fly in this kind of weather. They were considered the most powerful single-engine propeller planes ever designed.

More Transmissions

The next transmissions were confused. The operators listened to Taylor's frantic voice as he reported, "Both my compasses are out. . . ." Despite increasing static, a bit later the operators heard Taylor announce, "I'm sure I'm in the Keys [the chain of islands curving south and west of the Florida peninsula]. . . ." About 4:45 P.M. Taylor radioed that somehow Flight 19 had ended up over the Gulf of Mexico, far off course. About that time a storm front hit the area, bringing forty-knot winds, torrents of rain, and twelve-to-fourteen-foot waves. At 6:02 one of the Avengers radioed, "We may have to ditch any minute."

A 1991 *People* magazine story recounted the day's events. The writers, headed by Bill Hewitt, stated that

> experienced hands knew that ditching in such rough seas would be almost suicidal. Even if by

"In the 30 years from 1945 to 1975, [ships and aircraft] of all types, involving approximately 1,700 human beings—have vanished within the Bermuda Triangle without a shred of evidence to explain their loss."

Martin S. Caidin, *Fate*, January 1993

"[Some investigators] are not trying to find any explainable force. Some people like to drink from the fountain of knowledge. Others only gargle."

Author Lawrence Kusche, interviewed on *NOVA*, "The Case of the Bermuda Triangle," in 1988

Navy officials dispatched a Martin Mariner seaplane like this one to search for the wreckage of Flight 19. Mysteriously, it never returned to base.

with crew aboard

great luck the crews survived the initial impact and managed to break out their life rafts, they would, in all likelihood, be quickly capsized. Still, those at the base tried to remain hopeful.

A Martin Mariner seaplane with a crew well oriented in search and rescue operations headed out over the Atlantic. Several hours later they had found nothing. As darkness came on, limiting visibility, navy operators on the ground ordered the rescue plane back to base. They received no reply. The Martin Mariner never returned.

John Evans, a navy photographer, recalls that air traffic controllers lit up all the runways to guide the fliers home. "I'll never forget," says Evans, now in his sixties, "I went out around 9 o'clock, and the lights were still on. But then slowly, one by one, they all went out, and I thought, 'That's it, they're dead.'"

People reports that Coast Guard vessels continued to look for survivors during the night. At dawn the next day, one of the most intensive air-sea searches ever conducted began. Rescue teams on hundreds of planes, military ships, and privately owned boats searched the Atlantic, the Caribbean, and parts of the Gulf of Mexico. Dawn-to-dusk searches revealed no life rafts on the water and no airplane wreckage on the beaches of Florida or the Bahama Islands. Several weeks of searching proved fruitless. The five planes of Flight 19 had vanished.

So had the rescue plane.

It seemed impossible not only that experienced pilots would lose their bearings in good weather, but that a rescue plane would disappear also.

Corporal Kosnar, who had had "a premonition of danger," was lucky. Charles Berlitz, in *The Bermuda Triangle*, reports that he said, "I can't explain why, but . . . I decided not to go on the flight that day."

A Triangle of Danger

Thirty years after the tragedy of Flight 19, a rash of news stories again brought the incident to the public's attention. Accounts of other disappearances, both ships and planes, became a center of controversy. Investigators, scientific and unscientific, pondered the problem of what had now become known as the Bermuda Triangle.

Vincent H. Gaddis, a writer for *Argosy*, an adventure magazine, gave the area its popular name. In February 1964 he published an article entitled "The Deadly Bermuda Triangle." Gaddis described

Did Cpl. Allan Kosnar have a premonition about the fate of Flight 19?

an area where "total vanishments of ships and planes" occurred. According to Gaddis, the area could be defined by drawing a line from Florida to Bermuda, another from Bermuda to Puerto Rico, and a third back to Florida. This triangle includes the Bahama Islands. Other writers have extended the triangle farther into the Caribbean Sea on the southeast and beyond Bermuda to the north. Actually, if all disappearances are charted, the area resembles a trapezium, a four-sided figure in which no two sides or angles are the same. Other variations were a fan-shaped triangle and an open-sided triangle.

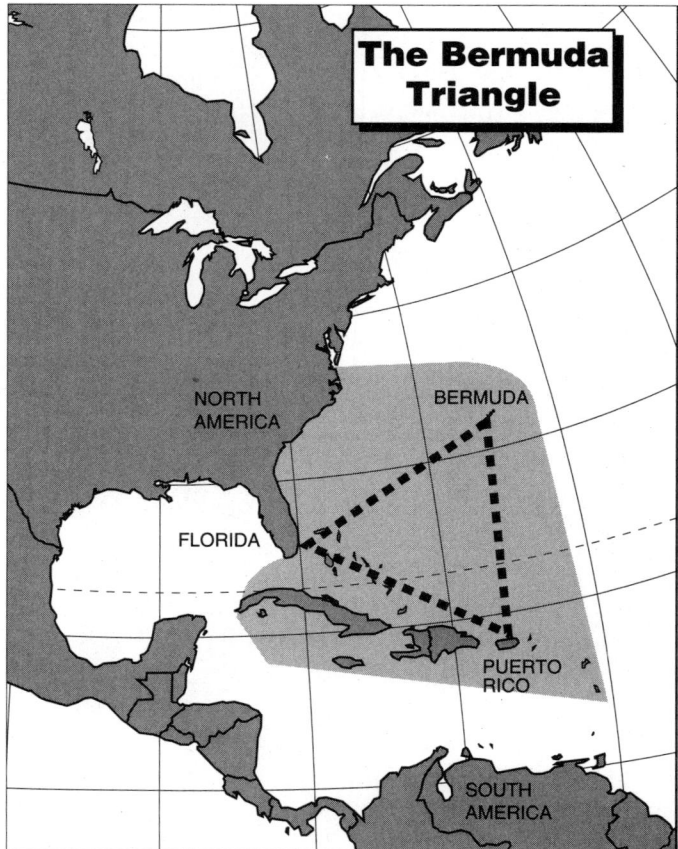

The Bermuda Triangle

Two popular views of the Bermuda Triangle. The dotted-line triangle represents Vincent H. Gaddis's original description of the area. Other writers have extended these boundaries, as represented by the shaded area.

Controversy began over which diagram was correct and, indeed, whether any such deadly area existed at all.

"The 'Bermuda Triangle,' or 'Devil's Triangle,' is a mythical geographic area," states a fact sheet issued by the U S. Coast Guard. The fact that the Coast Guard has made extensive, though futile, searches, the fact sheet says, has "lent credence to popular belief in the mysterious and supernatural qualities of the 'Bermuda Triangle.'" But, the fact sheet further states:

> The majority of disappearances can be attributed to the area's unique environmental features. . . . It is true that some exceptional magnetic values have been reported within the Triangle, but none to make the Triangle more unusual than any other place on earth.

Many scientists agree. They argue that *if all the facts were known*, each loss could be laid to one of three factors: natural events, human error, mechanical failure—or a combination of all three. Since so few facts *are* known, however, experts and amateurs have offered countless theories to explain the disappearances. Some of them have to do with the supernatural.

No Wreckage

"Large and small boats have disappeared without leaving wreckage, as if they and their crews had been snatched into another dimension," says Charles Berlitz. "Unexplained disappearances in the Bermuda Triangle have continued to the present day. . . . Something is very wrong with this area."

That "something" may include sudden tidal waves caused by earthquakes, ball lightning that strikes planes, making them explode, or gas leaks from the ocean bottom that cause shattering explosions, destroying low-flying aircraft.

A few people have attributed the mysterious disappearances to attacks by sea monsters. Some cite a

"Tragedies connected to this region continually occur without explanation, without pattern, without warning, and without reason."

Author John Wallace Spencer,
Limbo of the Lost

"The losses in the area referred to by Americans as the Bermuda Triangle must inevitably be chalked up to happenstance."

Insurance underwriter Leigh R. Hunt,
Lloyds of London

time warp leading to another dimension in space. Others have suggested that the cause is gravitational vortices, or whirlpools. Still others wonder whether unidentified flying objects (UFOs) operated by beings from ancient times, outer space, or even the future may play a role in the mystery.

Far-fetched Theories?

While some of these ideas may seem far-fetched, Charles Berlitz thinks that at the very least, there is more to the Bermuda Triangle mystery than is known today. He offers still another theory: that a four-hundred-foot-tall pyramid on the ocean floor releases electromagnetic forces powerful enough to cause the disintegration of people and vessels.

"Nonsense," says Ralph Stephen, a scientist at the Woods Hole Oceanographic Institution. "There's absolutely nothing scientific supporting the phenomenon [of the Bermuda Triangle]. There's nothing mysterious there."

It is not easy to separate fact from fantasy. One reason, Berlitz contends, is that pilots, airplane and

Could deadly sea monsters be responsible for the mysterious disappearances in the Bermuda Triangle?

fishing crews, and people living in the area of the Bermuda Triangle hesitate to talk about unusual experiences for "fear of ridicule, loss of credibility, or even from an inclination to believe that it is bad luck to talk about it."

Are there facts not yet uncovered, ideas not yet explored? Is the Bermuda Triangle legend based on fact, or is it a myth emerging from human fascination with the unknown?

Two

Out of the Past

(Opposite page) Navigators have long regarded the Bermuda Triangle as a perilous region. Many sailors from ancient times feared that fierce monsters lurked beneath the waves, waiting to attack boats and pull them to the bottom of the sea.

The waters off the east coast of the United States had a reputation for danger and mystery long before navigational charts were created. As long ago as 500 B.C., an admiral named Himilco, from the city of Carthage in North Africa, ventured far to the west, out into the Atlantic Ocean. There he encountered a strange and frightening place where his ship was becalmed for an unusually long time. In his log, Himilco wrote: "No breeze drives the ship, so dead is the sluggish wind of this idle sea. . . . There is much seaweed among the waves, it holds back the ship like bushes. . . . Fierce monsters swim among the . . . slowly creeping ships." He and his crew began to feel strangely haunted.

Carthaginian coins have been found off the coast of the United States. Historians use these coins to show that ships of ancient Carthage sailed into the waters of the Sargasso Sea. Himilco's ship was one of the lucky ones. It returned to Africa despite the terrors that were said to lurk in this area.

A Sea Within a Sea

The Sargasso Sea is an area with less wind, rain, and clouds than the rest of the Atlantic Ocean. It is not marked by shores, but instead stretches from 30

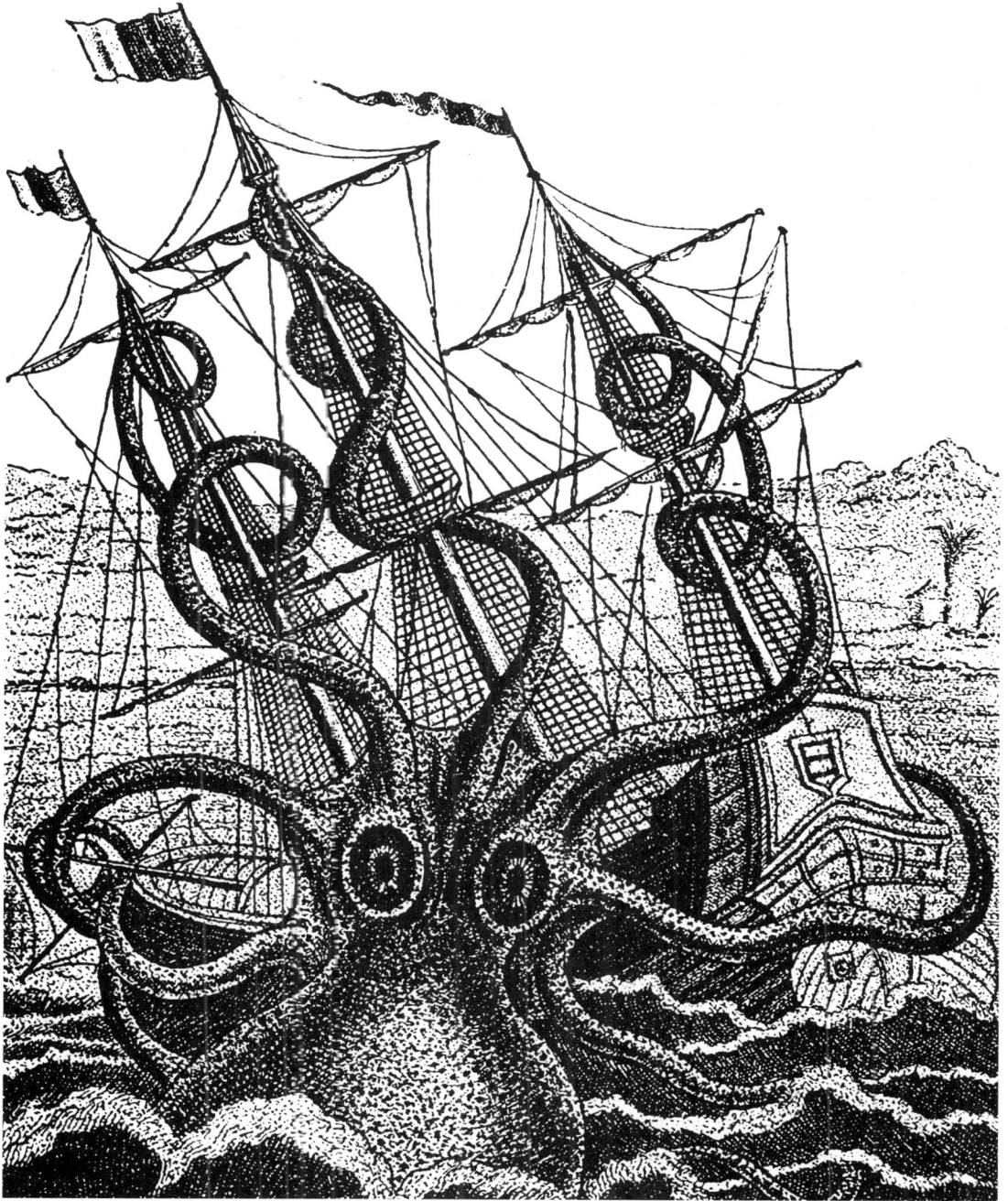

The Sargasso Sea, an area
of mystery and legend.

degrees to 70 degrees west longitude and from 20
degrees to 35 degrees north latitude. These coordi-
nates place it in the central part of the North Atlantic, east of Bermuda. The Sargasso Sea is slightly
smaller than the continental United States. More
than two thousand miles long and one thousand
miles wide, it is almost dead calm because a powerful current known as the Gulf Stream passes it to the
north, then swings around and returns from the
southwest. Thus, the Sargasso Sea is bounded on all
sides by currents, which cause its waters to rotate
slowly clockwise.

Great masses of sargasso, or gulfweed, form a
thick mat in this region of the Atlantic. Floating debris, such as tree trunks torn loose from riverbanks
by floods in Central America and the West Indies,
collects on the surface of the water. Oil from tankers

collects here, too. Plants drift in, adding to the mass and choking the waters. Debris of any sort that drifts into the relatively calm center of the Sargasso Sea usually remains until it sinks, rotating in slow, enormous circles.

In his book *The Bermuda Triangle Mystery—Solved*, Lawrence Kusche says, "The yellow, brown, and green seaweed crawling with strange creatures and extending as far as the eye could see was terrifying to those sailing through it." Commenting on legends of this sea, Kusche adds that "the thick mats of weed that supposedly grew up the sides of the ship, up the ropes and chains, [held the ships] fast under the hot sun until all aboard died of thirst or starvation and the ship became a rotted hull manned only by skeletons." In truth, borer worms, which thrive in tropical waters, sometimes *did* turn the sides of a becalmed ship into a putrid mess. No one knows how many rotted ships may have then slipped beneath the surface of this still sea.

Christopher Columbus

Christopher Columbus's voyages added to the air of mystery and danger in the area. He recorded in his log such sightings as a weed-filled sea, a great flame of fire, and strange lights in the night. In their versions of these stories, the crew transformed the little sea creatures that crept among the weeds into monsters and giant squid that could haul a ship down to the depths of the ocean. According to Kusche, "The rumor grew that crews often died an agonizing death because there was no air to breathe."

In his book *Is There a Bermuda Triangle?*, Michael J. Cusack says, "Writers have described the Sargasso Sea as a strange, frightening, mysterious place, teeming with life." But scientific studies have shown that it is almost a biological desert, with less food for sea creatures than anywhere else in the world. Still, Columbus's sailors were said to have

"When he entered this stretch of the Atlantic, Christopher Columbus noted curious glowing streaks of 'white water.' The mysterious patches of light and foam are still visible today and [are] so bright that they have been seen by U.S. astronauts from outer space."

"Graveyard of the Atlantic," *Newsweek*, December 16, 1974

"It's almost all hocey. Columbus never reported seeing white water in the area."

Historian Samuel Eliot Morison, *Time*, January 6, 1975

An artist's depiction of Columbus's voyage shows the seas swarming with mythical creatures.

sworn that monsters lived among the weeds. They were grey with fear.

Stories of the "horse latitudes" intensified that fear. The horse latitudes extend across the Atlantic Ocean, cutting through the Sargasso Sea. In the days of sailing ships, vessels carrying horses often became stranded in the region. After week upon rainless week at sea, supplies of drinking water grew dangerously low. Thirst-crazed horses occasionally broke loose and plunged into the ocean. Superstitious sailors believed that ghosts of the dead horses hovered close to the surface of the water.

So the stories grew. The tales intrigued Australian author and adventurer, Alan Villiers, who sailed into the Sargasso Sea in the early 1900s. In *Wild Ocean*, he writes:

> I kept a sharp lookout for ancient galleons and other derelicts [abandoned ships] lying unmanned upon the sea. At that time, there were derelicts to be encountered in the waters of the North Atlantic . . . drifting about sometimes for years. We saw nothing of these except one burning ship, which became a drifting and abandoned hulk. . . . Her crew took to their boats, and our four-masted bark wallowed there for many days.

Scientist and author Ivan T. Sanderson contends that the stories of this area are greatly exaggerated. In his book *Invisible Residents*, he states: "It is just possible, that small sailing vessels . . . in the very early days, may have been truly impeded by masses of floating seaweed." But he believes a properly rigged sailing ship, or a powered one, would have been able to "plow merrily through the mess."

Sargasso Sea

35°
HORSE LATITUDES
30°

Currents surrounding the Sargasso Sea cause its waters to rotate like a slow whirlpool, sucking floating debris to its center and choking the waters.

"Why do they all go unseen and in such silence? They cannot all slip suddenly beneath the sea like large stones, or just roll over and go straight on down."

Author Alan Villiers, *Posted Missing*

"I think the whole Bermuda Triangle mystique is hogwash. It's one of those mythic controversies that lingers on because it cannot be disproved."

Managing editor Patience Wales, *Sail* magazine, in a letter to Norma Gaffron, May 1986

Records show that for more than one hundred years, and perhaps longer than that, ships both large and small vanished in the region of the Sargasso Sea. These stories, like ghosts, float out of the mists of time. Some losses may be blamed on the characteristics of the area, but not all.

The disappearance of Flight 19 recalled to many researchers' minds stories of other mysterious happenings off the east coast of North America.

The Case of the Missing Crew

One of the earliest mysteries recorded was the loss of the crew of the *Rosalie*, a large French vessel. The ship was found a bit farther south than the area usually called the Bermuda Triangle, near Havana, Cuba. All sails were set and its cargo was intact. However, the crew was missing. An article published in the London *Times* on November 6, 1840, reported that the abandoned ship had been discovered in August of that year, and "the only living beings found on board were a cat, some fowls, and several canaries half dead with hunger." The valuable cargo, including wines, fruits, and silks, was in perfect condition. The captain's papers were all secure and in their proper places.

In an effort to solve the mystery of the lost crew of the *Rosalie*, author Lawrence Kusche investigated the incident. He found that another vessel, the *Rossini*, had run aground near Havana in August 1840. Kusche concluded that because the names of the ships were so similar, the editor of the London newspaper might have mistaken one name for the other, "especially if they were handwritten, which most messages were in 1840." Kusche then says, "It appears that the authorities . . . did not know that the vessel [the *Rossini*] had run aground two weeks before and that those on board had been rescued."

Still, there is no definite proof one way or the other, and the fate of the crew of the *Rosalie* is still a mystery.

Another loss, that of the English ship *Atalanta*, seemed especially tragic because the ship's crew consisted mainly of young sea cadets.

The *Atalanta*: A Ship That Never Returned

In January 1880, Her Majesty's Ship *Atalanta* set sail from the sunny shores of Bermuda. On board were 290 cadets, in training to be sailors. Many of the youths were relative novices.

The cadets had sailed to Barbados in the West Indies, then north, toward Bermuda. No doubt they were now anxious to return to their families, since the voyage had begun in England in November. Another reason for anxiety may have been the tales they had undoubtedly heard about the islands of Bermuda, which were labeled "Isles of the Devils" on ancient navigation charts.

The *Atalanta* was scheduled to return to its home port by March 1. When it was two weeks overdue, a search began. The Royal Navy combed

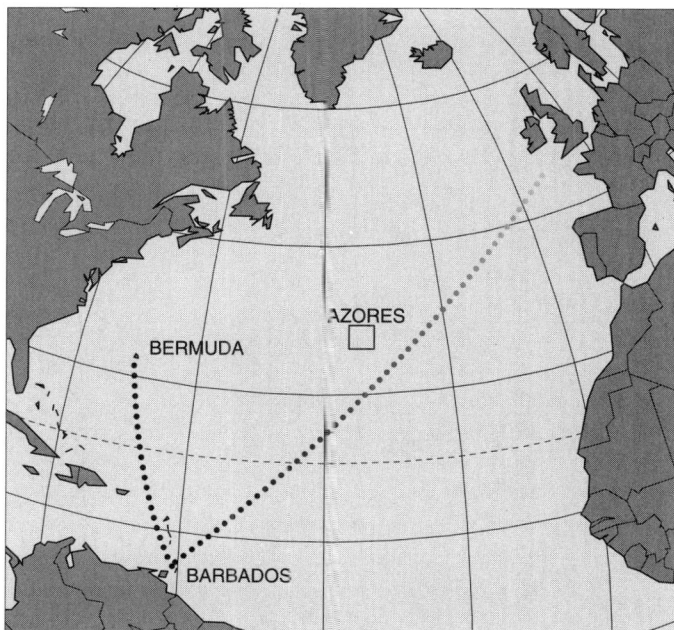

The route of the ill-fated *Atalanta*. Somewhere between the Azores and England, the British ship became another Bermuda Triangle mystery.

the sea between England and the Azores, islands that lie off the coast of Portugal, on the usual route for training ships. But the *Atalanta* had not been seen.

Crews of other ships scanned the seas, hoping for some sign of the *Atalanta*. They found nothing. During the next three months the London *Times* reported facts, opinions, theories, and fears about the fate of the ship. On April 14, 1880, the newspaper

Could turbulent storms have caused ships sailing through the Bermuda Triangle to perish?

stated that the *Atalanta* had left Bermuda carrying 109 tons of water and an ample supply of provisions. "The ship was in all respects sound, possessed of unusual stability, and commanded by an officer of good judgment and high professional qualifications," the *Times* stated. Because of the severe weather in the Atlantic Ocean in February and March, the editors feared the ship had lost its mast in a gale, but that did not mean it had sunk. They offered the hope that the *Atalanta* had been driven off her course and would still arrive home safely.

Other theories abounded. Maybe the ship had burned. Maybe it had drifted so far off course that it had collided with an iceberg. The *Times* stated that the coral reefs in the vicinity of Bermuda were extremely dangerous, and the *Atalanta* may have sailed no more than ten miles off its shores. In that case wreckage "would most probably drift out to sea and be carried eastwards by the Gulf Stream."

On April 27, a seaman named John Varling arrived in Portsmouth aboard the *Tamar*. Varling had been aboard the *Atalanta* but had left the ship before it sailed from Bermuda. Varling said the ship was "exceedingly crank, as being overweight," and that it rolled so much the captain feared it would founder (become disabled or sink). Varling further claimed that the officers, "with the exception of two, . . . were almost as much out for training as the crew." The work of shortening sail, he said, was left to the few able seamen on board. He said many of the young cadets were seasick.

Varling reported another significant detail: two men on board had died of yellow fever. Was it possible that *everyone* on board died of the disease?

Waiting for the *Atalanta*

Relatives of the cadets and officers aboard the luckless ship sent telegrams to the Navy Department and made personal visits to government officials asking for information. There was none to be had.

"Superstitions get started for a reason. People disappear here."

Character on *Sea Quest*, NBC television, November 7, 1993

"The Bermuda Triangle myth . . . was born on a slow news day in 1950."

"Lost Squadron," Time, May 27, 1991

The *Times* tried to reassure its readers that one vessel had taken eighty-four days to return from Bermuda: the *Atalanta* had been at sea for only seventy-four; therefore, families should not yet give up hope.

Several seafarers reported sightings of overturned vessels, but they proved to be ships other than the *Atalanta*. Stories of messages floating in bottles and carved on barrel staves gave false hope. None of the messages was authentic.

By April 21, 1880, the tone of the comments in the London newspaper had changed. The *Times* said:

> There can be no question of the criminal folly of sending some three hundred lads . . . [to sea] in a training ship without a sufficient number of trained and experienced seamen to take charge of her in exceptional circumstances. . . . When we consider that young lads are frequently afraid to go aloft in a gale to take down sail . . . a special danger attaching to the *Atalanta* becomes apparent.

By June 10, the accountant-general of the Royal Navy removed the name of the training ship from the navy list. Wives of officers were told they would receive special pensions as widows, since their husbands apparently had drowned in the performance of duty.

The *Atalanta* was never found.

Wrecked by Storms?

Almost a hundred years later, author and lecturer John Wallace Spencer wrote about the *Atalanta* in his book about the Bermuda Triangle, *Limbo of the Lost*. Spencer disagreed with the sailor Varling's appraisal of the situation. He said that a British investigating committee had considered the *Atalanta* a very stable ship and spoke favorably of the officers and crew. But, he added, the committee had pointed out that at the time of her loss, exceptional storms had sunk a number of merchant vessels. The committee thought storms must have caused the loss of the *Atalanta* as well. Spencer pointed out that one strange difference remained between the case of the *Atalanta* and the ships known to have been wrecked by the storms: in the other instances, survivors or debris always had been found.

Spencer stated that a British naval vessel like the *Atalanta* was much safer than a merchant ship. He concluded that the only sure fact is that the *Atalanta* sailed into the "limbo of the lost" and was never heard from again.

"It cannot be said with certainty that no trace of the ship was ever found," declares Lawrence Kusche. This author believes that unmarked masts, lifeboats, and wreckage considered to be parts of other ships could have come from the *Atalanta*.

This explanation would not have been easily accepted by parents waiting in 1880 on England's shores for a ship that never returned. They were more likely to have recalled the tales of terror told through the centuries, tales of ships lost in a place between Bermuda and the Azores called the Sargasso Sea.

No one knows whether supernatural forces had anything to do with the disappearance of 290 British cadets and their officers, but like a ghost from the past, the unsolved mystery of HMS *Atalanta* haunts us to this day.

Three

Nature and Its Tricks

(Opposite page) A ship, dwarfed by the ocean's expanse, heads away from ominous-looking water-spouts. Most experts believe that disappearances in the Bermuda Triangle are most likely due to natural forces.

Is there really a mysterious Bermuda Triangle that swallows ships and planes?

"No," says Michael J. Cusack. "Not if we mean a patch of ocean where uncanny forces are at work." But, he adds, "Yes, if we mean a place where ships and planes can be suddenly and unexpectedly overcome by the forces of nature."

According to Cusack, this region of the sea has many complex and varied hazards. Furthermore, he says, "The source of the danger can be so localized that no one but the victims may be aware of it when it actually strikes."

Most scientists believe that disappearances in this area, as well as in other parts of the ocean, are most likely due to natural but unusual occurrences. The U.S. Coast Guard, responsible for investigating shipwrecks and disappearances, agrees. According to one of their official statements: "The majority of disappearances can be attributed to the area's unique environmental features. These include raging storms, strong currents, waterspouts, and mysterious forces yet to be understood."

Between June and December, one of these natural forces—hurricanes—rages in the western Atlantic. Hurricanes usually form when the sun is di-

A satellite photo of a hurricane formation off the coast of Florida. Early navigators did not understand the nature of hurricanes and could not always predict a storm's arrival.

rectly overhead and the sea surface is warm. Water evaporates rapidly from a particularly warm patch of ocean, and the moisture-laden air rises. Then cooler, denser air swirls in to replace the rising air. The cool air is warmed and rises also. Thus a spiral is created, and it keeps spinning: warmed air rises; cool air takes its place. The cycle speeds up, and the spiral moves faster and faster.

Rain falls, causing the spinning air to cool even more rapidly. The heat energy that is released adds fury to the storm. The result: a deadly hurricane.

The winds of a hurricane swirl in a counterclockwise direction. Hurricanes themselves tend to travel clockwise. Extremely varied ocean and climatic conditions make it difficult to predict exactly where a hurricane will form, but most killer storms develop off the west coast of Africa, acquiring hurricane status in the West Indies, the Gulf of Mexico, or the Caribbean Sea. Hurricanes tend to move through the Bermuda Triangle.

In the early days of sea travel, voyagers did not have scientific knowledge of the nature of storms.

Thus the more competent mariners developed a keen "weather eye." For example, after several trips to the New World, Christopher Columbus became aware of signs of bad weather in this part of the new world. In 1502 he sheltered his ships in a harbor on Hispaniola, the island that contains the nations known today as Haiti and the Dominican Republic. His wisdom saved him, while twenty-six ships of a less-observant treasure fleet captain were caught in a hurricane and destroyed.

Meteorologists (weather scientists) today give early warning of hurricanes and chart storm progress daily, even hourly. Careful voyagers use this information to change their schedules and routes to avoid disaster. But lesser storms come without warning, and many of them are violent enough to destroy pleasure boats, fishing vessels, or small airplanes.

Even when a ship survives, the crew of a vessel that has been peppered all night with bolt after bolt of lightning can come ashore badly shaken and with reason to be terrified of the forces found in the Triangle.

Balls of Fire

Some sailors report a phenomenon even more spectacular than hurricanes: ball lightning. Francis Hitching, in *The Mysterious World, An Atlas of the Unexplained*, defines ball lightning as "a self-contained bright light, usually spherical but sometimes pear-shaped at the edges and in a variety of colours . . . [that] hovers, bounces, or moves erratically about before disappearing." It moves slowly and may last for several seconds or several minutes. Sometimes it scorches objects it touches. Sometimes it explodes in the air. According to Hitching, "There is no accepted scientific explanation for these balls of fire." Although many scientists think ball lightning (often called fireballs) is not harmful, an incident recounted by Hitching shows that this is not always true.

"In most cases, there were no distress calls and no indications of trouble. Whatever had happened must have happened very quickly. In many instances, the last reports stated that all was well."

Author Elwood D. Baumann, *The Devil's Triangle*

"Would not a captain and his crew, in the face of a severe storm or other emergency, be reluctant to admit there was something they could not handle? We think it reasonable that, in some cases, a show of pride may have delayed calling for help until it was too late."

Charles J. Cazeau and Stuart D. Scott Jr., *Exploring the Unknown: Great Mysteries Reexamined*

A nineteenth-century illustration depicts farm workers reacting with terror after a close call with a scorching-hot fireball. Although many scientists believe ball lightning is not usually harmful, when it hits sea vessels carrying inflammable fuel it can be deadly.

In the Midlands of England, Hitching says, "A young housewife was in the kitchen of her home . . . when a sphere of light appeared. . . . It was about ten centimetres [four inches] across, and surrounded by a flame-colored halo; its color was bright blue to purple." The ball moved straight toward the woman, and she brushed it away. Where her hand touched the fireball, a redness and swelling appeared on her left hand. "It seemed as if my gold wedding ring was burning into my finger," she said. The ball disappeared with a bang, and scorched a small hole in the woman's skirt, but she was otherwise unharmed.

The effects of fireballs when they hit highly inflammable fuel can be lethal. Trucks, barges, and

St. Elmo's fire glows from the mast of a ship sailing through rough waters. This strange phenomenon is unlikely to cause harm.

tankers have exploded after contact with ball lightning.

Another rare electrical discharge is a brilliant light known as St. Elmo's fire. It resembles a flame and is sometimes seen at prominent points such as a mast on a ship at sea. Observers have been badly frightened, but not harmed, by this strange light. Most experts, then, doubt that mysterious phenomena like St. Elmo's fire have caused Bermuda Triangle disappearances. They do concede, however, that unusual weather certainly accounts for some disappearances. Still, again and again, accounts of mysterious losses begin with the words, "The sky was clear and blue, the sea was calm." Then too, storms rarely occur in this area in December, January, February, and March, yet winter is the season when the menace that seems to haunt the Bermuda Triangle often strikes. It appears to have struck a British passenger plane, the *Star Tiger*, en route from London to Havana, Cuba, just three years after the disappearance of Flight 19.

The *Star Tiger*

In the early morning hours of January 30, 1948, an all-metal Tudor IV monoplane, the *Star Tiger*, disappeared after having radioed its position to the air traffic control tower at Bermuda. After a lengthy investigation, the British Ministry of Civil Aviation issued a report stating that "Up to 3 A.M. on January 30th, . . . it is a reasonable inference from the known facts that *Star Tiger* had had a steady and uneventful flight. Her officers had received and acknowledged the Bermuda weather forcasts."

Furthermore, the report stated, "In the vicinity of the last known position of *Star Tiger*, and in any area in which she is likely to have flown thereafter, the weather was stable." The board of inquiry eliminated other possible causes of trouble such as fire, loss of engine power, and structural defects. The panelists said that "no more baffling problem has ever been presented [to the board] for investigation." They added that in some cases, "some external cause may overwhelm both man and machine. What happened in this case will never be known and the fate of *Star Tiger* must forever remain an unsolved mystery."

In spite of the extensive report from the British authorities, author Lawrence Kusche insists that the weather was deteriorating during the latter stages of the flight; he says also that winds were increasing, and he points out that the aircraft's supply of fuel would have been diminishing.

Kusche, like the U.S. Coast Guard, believes that weather is the cause of most of the losses in the Triangle. He cites another example, the case of the *Revonoc*. When this forty-five-foot racing yacht vanished in Florida waters on January 6, 1958, there were, according to the *New York Times*, "wind-lashed seas off the southern coast of Florida." But those who knew the captain of the boat were sure that the storm was not severe enough to have sunk the *Revonoc*. A family friend, Richard Bertram, said, "Harvey Conover [the skipper and owner of the yacht] was too good a sailor to let that happen to him."

No one knows what happened to the *Revonoc*.

What *is* known is that winds blow all the time in this region of the Atlantic Ocean. The prevailing

According to Harvey Conover's friends, Conover was an experienced skipper who knew how to sail in inclement weather. They are not convinced that a storm alone was responsible for the disappearance of his racing yacht the *Revonoc*, shown here.

tropical winds are from the northeast, from the vicinity of the European landmass. When these winds approach the continent of Africa, they turn west to howl across the vast, open reaches of the Atlantic. In the old days sailors intent on trading in America dubbed these movements of air the northeast trade winds, which they are still called today. The traders were happy to take advantage of them.

Similarly, airflow south of the equator constitutes the southeast trade winds. Between these two wind patterns is an area of calm called the doldrums. North and south of the doldrums, trade winds force water westward, creating currents that influence weather and sea conditions.

Not only are these currents pushed along by the trade winds, they are also pulled by the earth's rotation. Warm and swift waters from north and south meet and merge. Currents split, then join, then combine with other currents to create mighty rushes of water that swirl around boats and small ships.

Currents may be indirectly responsible for some losses of aircraft and ships. When warm waters hit the colder waters of the Atlantic Ocean, fog frequently forms. If a boat or plane were to become hopelessly lost in a dense fog, its crew might panic. Then the plane might plunge deep into the ocean, the ship crash against unseen rocks or a deserted coastline. But why, in such cases, are there no calls for help, no bodies washed ashore, and no wreckage?

The Gulf Stream

Some experts point out that the swift current of the Gulf Stream quickly carries debris away from accident sites. The Gulf Stream is an especially treacherous area of the Atlantic Ocean where currents merge. As science writer Cusack says, the Gulf Stream is a sort of river within the ocean, which flows from the Caribbean, north past Florida, Georgia, South Carolina, and North Carolina. It is particularly swift as it surges past Florida, as well as

"What possible explanations can there be for these sudden accidents? There are indications that some powerful and as yet unknown physical force is at work in the Bermuda Triangle."

Author Robert F. Burgess, *Sinkings, Salvages, and Shipwrecks*

"The 'evidence'. . . may be a mixture of myths, unsubstantiated reports, and half-truths. The only thing that seems to be certain is that the Bermuda Triangle is a controversial subject."

"The Bermuda Triangle and the Earth's Magnetism," fact sheet from the National Oceanic and Atmospheric Administration

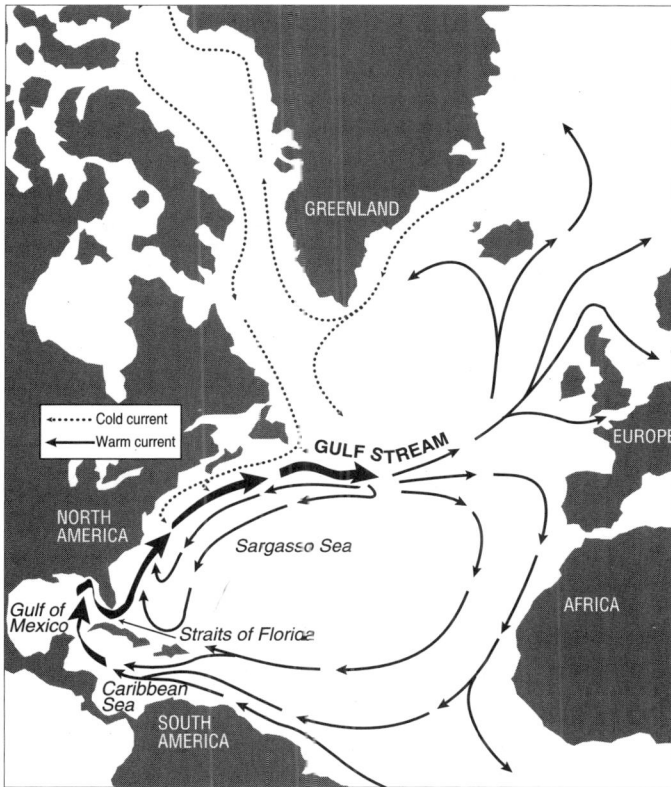

Arrows illustrate how the Gulf Stream merges with cold and warm currents, creating a treacherous area of the ocean that can carry ships adrift.

particularly concentered. It is about forty-eight miles wide and twenty-one hundred feet deep. Farther north the Gulf Stream turns eastward. It becomes wider, shallower, and cooler. And less dangerous.

Authorities in marinas along the coast of the southeastern United States urge vacationers in small craft to take Gulf Stream currents into account as they prepare to sail to the Bahama Islands. If they plot their course without considering the current— ordinarily three to four knots (about 3.5-4.5 miles per hour)—they may never reach their destination. The Gulf Stream can carry unwary sailors far off course. Likewise, it could carry debris many, many miles from the site of a wreck, far beyond the areas rescue workers would logically search.

However, the Gulf Stream is not the only aspect of the Triangle area that wise sailors fear.

Deepwater Eddies

One day in 1944 a ship named the *Caicos Trader* towed a fishing boat, the *Wild Goose*, over an extremely deep part of the ocean near the Bahama Islands. According to author Edward F. Dolan Jr., in *The Bermuda Triangle and Other Mysteries of Nature*, "Suddenly something went wrong. The fishing boat pitched upwards. Then it put its nose down. Finally it vanished beneath the water. The crew of the *Caicos Trader* quickly cut the towline before this strange force could pull their own ship under."

Luckily, Joe Talley, captain of the fishing boat, swam to the surface and was rescued. No one else had been aboard. The crew of the *Trader* later said that the *Wild Goose* "looked as if it had been caught in a whirlpool." They could have been right, for whirlpools come in many sizes, shapes, and energy levels.

Tiny whirlpools can be seen in country streams and along curbs and gullies. They catch leaves and pull them along, often down to the bottom of the stream. Whirlpools are more powerful and more frightening in the ocean. There, scientists call them eddies.

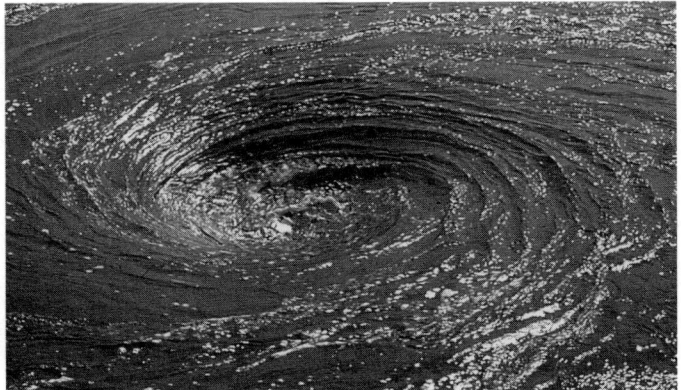

Powerful whirlpools that form in the ocean are known as eddies. Researchers disagree as to whether deepwater eddies are a serious hazard to boats and ships.

Eddies are wild, whirling currents of water that rush away from major ocean currents. Scientists have long known about the eddies that occur on or near the sea's surface. But in 1959 a British oceanographer, Dr. John Swallow, made a dramatic discovery. To measure the flow of deep currents in the western Atlantic, he had set out floats, free to drift at various levels beneath the sea's surface. Some of the deepwater floats drifted as Swallow had expected. Others swirled off in surprising directions. The maverick floats, which moved ten times faster than the others, were caught in *underwater* whirpools. Swallow had discovered a secret of the sea—deepwater eddies.

The British scientist theorized that deepwater eddies may be a factor in undersea storms, violent movements of water layers in the ocean depths. Highly energetic eddies spin away from the Gulf Stream into the Sargasso Sea, where they give up most of their energy to the atmosphere and to the surrounding ocean waters. Deepwater eddies are a threat to deep-diving submarines. Might they also threaten ships on the surface?

Scientists from Woods Hole Oceanographic Institution do not think so. They studied a three-hundred-mile circle of the ocean and discovered an enormous variety of eddies in the Bermuda Triangle. But these researchers found no evidence that eddies are a threat to surface vessels.

The crew of the *Caicos Trader* might be inclined to disagree.

Many other sea and weather conditions are candidates for blame in the many losses of ships, aircraft, and people in the Triangle area. Among them are waterspouts, tsunami waves, and dangerous gas deposits that leak from under the sea.

Waterspouts

Whereas an eddy is a whirlpool, or vortex, in the sea, a waterspout is a vortex in the air. Waterspouts occur frequently over the ocean between Florida and Bermuda.

These fast-moving vortices, often called wet tornadoes, are rapidly rotating air funnels, full of mist and moisture. Waterspouts extend downward from storm clouds to the surface of a body of water. Their whirling winds can reach a speed of one hundred miles per hour.

A waterspout may last no more than ten minutes, yet its force can rip apart a small ship, a boat, or a plane.

Tsunami Waves

The dangers seem endless. The U.S. Coast Guard offers the following warnings: "The unpredictable Caribbean-Atlantic storms that give birth to

Whirling air funnels called waterspouts are forceful enough to demolish a small plane or ship.

Tempestuous waves can pose a deadly threat to sea vessels.

waves of great size . . . often spell disaster for pilots and mariners." But seafarers have to worry not only about normal storm waves, but also waves that are the result of happenings *beneath* the sea.

The most powerful of these are tsunamis, waves that can build up speeds to six hundred miles per hour. Created by underwater earthquakes, tsunamis start out as long, low waves that become charging giants as they hit shallow water. Tsunami waves one hundred feet high have been reported. Since the waves build in deep water, they cannot be seen from the air, and they cannot be felt aboard a large ship in very deep water. But they pose a great danger to small ships and pleasure craft near shore, which can be swamped and crushed by the force of the pounding water.

Of lesser force are seiche waves, the products of underwater landslides caused by the pulling apart of the earth's crust.

Ironically, despite the dangers, smaller ships stand a greater chance than larger ships of surviving either tsunami or seiche waves. The smaller ships

Do undersea gas leaks explain the mystery of the Bermuda Triangle?

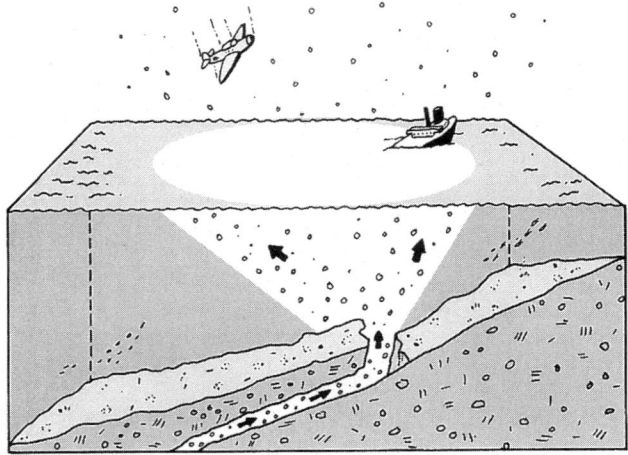

may ride over the crest of one wave and down in the trough between it and the next. But a large destroyer, whose length extends a trough and a half, could be broken in two.

Since waves such as these are most dangerous near shore, they could be responsible for the disappearances of some boats within sight of land. These would not be mysterious disappearances, however, since weather observers on land would certainly be aware of huge waves in their vicinity.

Gas Leaks

One more force from beneath the sea that may pose a threat to vessels and aircraft involves deposits of gas trapped at the bottom of the sea. An article in the November 1982 issue of *GEO* magazine contains the following statement by oil-industry consultant Richard McIver: "Violent plumes of gas escaping from pools of natural gas under the ocean floor might well be responsible for mysterious disappearances of ships and low-flying airplanes, such as those lost in the Bermuda Triangle."

Janice Nurski, writing in *Nature Canada*'s summer 1985 issue, explains how this occurs. In an article titled "Frozen Fuel," Nurski says, "Enormous pressures and low temperatures at the sea bottom shape water and gas molecules into gas hydrates, unique structures that resemble ice." Unlike ordinary ice, however, the water molecules that compose hydrates bond together in a three-dimensional network of spherical cages. They trap neighboring gas molecules, such as methane, formed from organic sediment deposited over millions of years. This combination of gases and water is a powerful reservoir of energy. It is colorless and odorless.

According to Richard McIver, "If the domelike seal over an undersea reservoir of gas were ruptured—by drilling, seismic [earthquakelike] tremor, a rise in temperature, or another disturbance—an enormous volume of gas could escape." The gas would burst upward, breaking into smaller and smaller bubbles as it neared the surface. A ship sailing into this area of frothy, gaseous water, lighter than the surrounding water, would suddenly lose buoyancy and sink. If the gas flow were large enough, a highly inflammable bubble of gas would shoot into the air, where it could cause engine failure in low-flying planes that encountered it.

McIver points out that conditions that would permit such disastrous sequences of events are found "off the southeast coast of the United States, the location of the Bermuda Triangle."

Glowing White Streaks

Information such as this sheds new light on a phenomenon reportedly observed by Columbus's crew: Charles Berlitz says that these mariners saw "curious glowing streaks of white water." An aerial photo showing luminous white streaks in the water off Orange Cay in the Bahamas appears in Berlitz's book *The Bermuda Triangle*. He describes them as "mysterious patches of light and foam." The astronauts of *Apollo 12* also observed streaks of light as they looked down from outer space. Perhaps the

"A possible theory may be some kind of atmospheric aberration—a phenomenon that might be called 'a hole in the sky.'"

Author Vincent H. Gaddis, *Invisible Horizons*

"It is not felt that an atmospheric aberration exists in this area."

Captain E.W. Humphrey, aviation safety coordinator

frothy, gaseous water bubbling up from gas leaks accounts for what had earlier been considered a mystery—even a supernatural occurrence. So far, this is only conjecture. No disappearances in the Bermuda Triangle have been blamed on gas leaks.

But other conditions—invisible ones—*have* been cited as possible factors in unexplained air disasters. It is impossible to ignore the strong and variable winds that blow almost constantly over the sea and the islands off Florida's east coast.

Hazardous Winds

In the early days of aviation, when adventuresome pilots pioneered overwater flight, many small

Pilots have reported seeing mysterious streaks of white water. Might they be something as ordinary as boat trails?

Wind shear may have been a factor in the explosion of the space shuttle *Challenger*. Is wind shear the terrible force that claims boats and planes in the Bermuda Triangle?

planes were lost, and these losses were not unexpected. But as planes improved, pilots gained experience, and radio and navigation instruments became more reliable, losses were no longer taken for granted.

Now, when thorough investigations reveal no obvious cause for the disappearance of aircraft of any size, meteorologists look for fatal factors in the sky. It has been discovered that on otherwise ordinary days, an ascending or descending aircraft can encounter strong winds, or turbulence, at different levels. Intense winds can move through the skies at speeds exceeding two-hundred miles per hour. Sudden changes in wind speed or direction present an invisible risk to air crews and passengers. Such a sudden change is called wind shear. Authorities cited wind shear as a possible factor in the explosion of the space shuttle *Challenger* on January 28, 1986.

William P. Birkemeier, who teaches engineering at the University of Wisconsin at Madison, studied atmospheric data for the day the shuttle left the launching pad at Cape Canaveral. He noted that the craft's entry and exit from a wind shear zone sixty seconds into its flight resulted in a seventy-mile-per-hour change in speed. This may have put too much pressure on the shuttle booster, causing the explosion.

Birkemeier said the leak in *Challenger*'s right solid fuel rocket booster corresponded with its entry into the wind shear. Four-tenths of a second later, the shuttle broke through the shear into calm air and winds of fourteen miles per hour.

"It would appear that the booster leak was caused by the sudden deceleration of the rocket as it flew through the shear zone," Birkemeier said, in an Associated Press story that appeared in the *Minneapolis Star and Tribune* on March 28, 1986.

Seven astronauts lost their lives in this tragedy.

Perhaps wind shear, not fully understood in the past, caused the *Star Tiger* to vanish in 1948. Perhaps, too, extremely variable winds claimed the *Star Ariel*, sister ship of the *Star Tiger*, in 1949. Both aircraft are still listed as victims of unknown forces.

Electromagnetism

Strong ocean currents, underwater earthquakes, waterspouts, and hazardous winds may explain some of the mysterious disappearances of ships and planes in the Bermuda Triangle. But pilots, navigators, and sailors report many other mysterious occurrences as well, such as compasses that rotate wildly, radio transmission failures, and shutdowns of entire electrical systems. Some sources say that the earth is awash in many kinds of energy, which scientists understand only partially. One of these—magnetism—may cause the puzzling events in the Bermuda Triangle.

A magnetic field surrounds the earth. The strength of this field is not constant, however; it shows irregular changes in direction and intensity, and it varies in different places on the earth's surface. In addition, the earth itself is an enormous permanent magnet. Francis Hitching writes in *The Mysterious World* that scientists describe the source of the earth's magnetism as "a giant bar magnet at the core of our planet" with the magnet's ends roughly at the North and South poles. However, the magnetic poles of the earth do not correspond *exactly* to the geographical poles. Nor do they control the compasses used on ships and planes.

Compass needles point to *magnetic* north, not so-called *true* north (the North Pole). This is because the controlling force is the earth's magnetic field. However, one of the few facts established about the Bermuda Triangle is that compass needles there point to *true* north.

The only other place on earth where the needle of a compass points to true north is off the coast of Japan, an area that is referred to as the Devil's Sea. Unexplained disappearances have occurred there also.

Navigators use the term "compass variation" to refer to the difference between true north and magnetic north. Variation changes as much as twenty degrees as one travels around the earth. Variation also changes annually, much as tides change with the seasons. These facts pose no problem for trained sailors and aviators, who routinely use charts that indicate variation changes. By consulting the charts, navigators can calculate their positions and their courses correctly.

Compass Irregularities

Problems occur when a marine or aviation compass does not behave in a normal manner. Compass irregularities have been reported again and again by fliers and sailors in the Bermuda Triangle. Many of these reports come from people experienced in their professions. Charles Lindbergh, the first pilot to

To stay on course, navigators routinely check charts for changes in "compass variation."

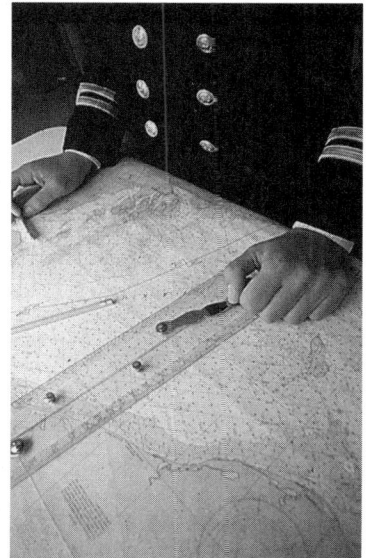

Charles Lindbergh reported compass irregularities while flying over the Bermuda Triangle.

solo nonstop across the Atlantic, flew over the ocean southeast of Florida one year after his historic flight. On this later flight, in 1928, Lindbergh noted that both of his compasses malfunctioned.

In 1966 Don Henry, captain of the salvage tugboat *Good News*, reported a disturbing incident while returning to Fort Lauderdale from Puerto Rico. His ship was towing a barge on a line a thousand feet behind the tug. Captain Henry says:

> It was afternoon, the weather was good, and the sky was clear. I had gone to the cabin for a few minutes when I heard a lot of hollering going on. . . . The first thing I looked at was the compass, which was spinning clockwise. There was no reason that this should ever happen—the

only place besides here I ever heard it to happen was in the St. Lawrence River . . . where a big deposit of iron or maybe a meteorite on the bottom makes the compasses go crazy.

Then, Captain Henry says, "The horizon disappeared. . . . The water, sky, and horizon all blended together." The barge the *Good News* was towing was hidden by a milky cloud, and around it the waves danced in confusion. The ship lost power, and as Captain Henry grabbed the rope and pulled the barge out of the cloud, he says, "It seemed that something wanted to pull us back, but it couldn't quite make it."

Yellow Hazes

Other sailors and fliers have reported yellow hazes, as well as the milky sort of cloud or fog that Captain Henry reported. Whether these incidents are in any way connected to magnetic fields is impossible to judge. Seasoned flier Martin S. Caidin thinks they are.

While Caidin was flying from Bermuda to Jacksonville, Florida, on June 11, 1986, his magnetic instruments ceased to function. At the same time, he says, a creamy yellow fog, the consistency of eggnog, surrounded his plane, leaving

> a narrow-diameter "hole" [through which he and the others aboard] could look straight up to see blue sky, and if we looked straight down . . . there was the ocean. It was as if a long pipe extended from the surface to the sky above, providing this keyhole of vision, and the pipe sped along with the airplane.

Reporting on this event in *Fate* magazine in January 1993, Caidin says, "The engines roared perfectly, . . . but we were no longer in any world we knew." Caidin and his passengers, who were all pilots, took turns flying the plane by aiming at the brightest area of the horizon, until—four hours later—the thick yellow fog disappeared.

Martin S. Caidin may have flown his plane through a bizarre magnetic storm over the Bermuda Triangle that caused his magnetic instruments to fail.

Caidin says, "The single explanation that appears to make sense is that the [plane] was enveloped, or was affected by, an intense electromagnetic field that dumped the instruments and 'blanked out' the electronic equipment."

Vincent H. Gaddis, in his book *Invisible Horizons*, speculates that magnetic storms may cause these mysterious compass disorders and the strange creamy yellow clouds that occasionally accompany them. A magnetic storm is a strong fluctuation in the earth's magnetic field. Such storms are caused by high-energy particles in the atmosphere and intense radiation given off as a result of solar activity. Magnetic storms cause disturbances in the ionosphere that interfere with shortwave radio reception.

Caidin (left) and Capt. Art Ward fly over the mid-Atlantic in 1986. Was it fate that allowed them to escape the doom of the Bermuda Triangle?

Perhaps, says Gaddis, such a storm interfered with the transmissions on Flight 19, causing the five navy bombers to lose contact with their base in Fort Lauderdale. He suggests that magnetic disturbances may also cause an abnormal atmospheric condition that creates "a hole in the sky." Planes could fly into such a place and never return, he says.

Electrical engineer Hugh Auchincloss Brown believes incidents involving compasses that spin wildly may be connected not to magnetic storms, but to changes in the earth's magnetic field. He suggests that "occasional magnetic 'earthquake' indications" may cause shifting in the magnetic field, which in turn cause compasses to misbehave.

Captain Henry's suggestion of a meteorite under the St. Lawrence River is similar to a theory proposed by Charles Berlitz as the cause of instrument failure off the southeast coast of Florida. In his book *Atlantis, the Eighth Continent*, Berlitz points out that a magnetic asteroid or meteorite could have collided with the earth in the distant past. If that happened, Berlitz says, and the object were still lying under the sea in the Bermuda Triangle, it could cause magnetic and communication problems.

Magnetism, with its incompletely understood effects, is a force scientists continue to study.

"There have been many incidences of compass needles spinning wildly for no apparent reason on vessels or aircraft passing through the 'triangle.'"

Author Richard Winer, *The Devil's Triangle*

"As far as NOAA's records are concerned, the Bermuda Triangle would seem to be relatively undisturbed, magnetically speaking."

William A. Stanley, administrator for the National Oceanic and Atmospheric Administration

Four

More Mysteries, More Explanations

(Opposite page) Some think that mysterious, unexplained forces cause the loss of ships in the Bermuda Triangle.

The weather was good and hurricane season was months away when a navy supply ship disappeared in the last year of World War I. USS *Cyclops*, a steamship 542 feet long, one of the largest vessels afloat, left the Caribbean island of Barbados in the early evening of March 4, 1918. Twenty-four hours later it exchanged messages with another ship, the liner *Vestris*. According to John Harris, author of *Without a Trace*, the *Cyclops* reported that the weather was fair and "made no mention of any trouble or difficulty. After that there was nothing."

The *Cyclops* was due in Norfolk, Virginia, on March 13. It never arrived. On April 15, the *Virginian-Pilot* newspaper ran a story that included a statement by the U.S. Navy Department: "No well-founded reason can be given to explain the *Cyclops* being overdue, as no radio communication with or trace of her has been had since leaving the West Indies Port." The navy confirmed that the weather in the area through which the vessel must have passed had "not been bad." Authorities knew that one of the ship's two engines was not operating and that the *Cyclops* was proceeding at reduced speed. But even if both engines had been totally disabled, its radio should not have been prevented from operating.

Yet no SOS ever came from the *Cyclops*.

Since this was wartime, the first theory offered to explain the ship's disappearance was that a torpedo had sunk it. But the navy stated that "while a raider or submarine could be responsible for her loss, there have been no reports that would indicate the presence of either in the locality." Besides, the Germans usually announced the destruction of large ships to demoralize their enemies. They made no such announcement about the *Cyclops*.

After the war ended, interest in the fate of the *Cyclops* and its crew continued. An American admiral, William S. Sims, searched German naval files and found that no German U-boats (submarines), surface vessels, or mines had been located where the *Cyclops* would have been steaming.

Though theories abound, no convincing evidence exists to explain the disappearance of the *Cyclops*.

The captain of the lost ship, Lt. Comdr. George Worley, had come to the United States from Germany as a child. Although Worley had become an American citizen in 1893, some people questioned his loyalty to his new country. Could he have been in sympathy with the Germans and surrendered the ship to them? Author John Harris calls this a silly suggestion. Even if Worley had been inclined to surrender the ship, it "could never have dodged the British and American blockading patrols."

A reporter for the *Literary Digest* interviewed the captain's wife in an article for that magazine's June 8, 1918, issue. The reporter quoted Mrs. Worley: "Do you think my husband would prove a traitor to America, to his wife and little daughter?" she asked. "My husband was an American through and through. . . . He came here seeking freedom and he would fight and die to maintain that freedom." Mrs. Worley believed that the vessel had been disabled at sea and that her husband and his crew were waiting to be picked up.

The disappearance of this huge ship, with 309 men aboard, became an intriguing mystery. The list of possible explanations grew long. Some of the theories could apply to other ships and planes as well as to the *Cyclops*. A popular theory was that the ship's cargo caused it to sink.

Improper Loading

Experts say that if heavy, bulky loads, such as the manganese ore the *Cyclops* carried, are not properly distributed, they can cause a ship to roll heavily. In high seas, a rolling ship could "turn turtle" and be unable to right itself.

Conrad Nervig, an ensign on board the *Cyclops*, watched the loading of the ship just before he received orders to join another vessel. In a paper published by the U.S. Naval Institute in 1969, Nervig expressed the opinion that the cargo might have been unevenly distributed. Richard Winer, author of

"For some four hours, what happened to us, as any sober scientist or engineer will tell you without a moment's hesitation, was and is absolutely impossible."

Author and sailor Martin S. Caidin, *Fate*, January 1993

"I keep an open mind on most things—but when it comes to the Bermuda Triangle, I feel there is no reason to believe there's anything mysterious out there."

Jim Bestul, former U.S. Navy pilot based in Bermuda, in conversation with Norma Gaffron, October 1993

Some experts warn that improper loading can cause a ship to roll heavily.

The Devil's Triangle, says the "ship was known to be overloaded," thus lending support to Nervig's theory.

But Lawrence Kusche disagrees. He says, "The ship . . . had been properly loaded. It was done under the personal supervision of Captain Worley and foreman Manuel Pereira . . . who had been in charge of loading vessels for many years."

Navy personnel thought the cargo, while properly loaded, might have shifted. Steel derricks, designed for loading and discharging cargo, towered above the vessel's deck. With this top-heavy equipment, strong winds, and shifting cargo, who knows what might have happened?

But no strong winds were reported.

The navy considered other possibilities.

Explosion or Collision

The Office of Naval Intelligence theorized that the *Cyclops* may have exploded. However, Winer says that the ship was not heavily enough armed for this to be likely. Also, not a speck of wreckage from the *Cyclops* was ever found.

Explosions have been considered in other cases as well. Some experts suggest such a fate for the Mariner rescue craft that was lost while looking for Flight 19 in 1945. In a 1988 *NOVA* video, "The Case of the Bermuda Triangle," Richard Adams, who had been in charge of the Flight 19 rescue mission, stated that the Mariner carried so much high-octane fuel that they were "potential flying bombs." Fumes collected in the planes, he said.

The Martin Mariner that vanished while searching for Flight 19 carried a large volume of high-octane fuel, leading some experts to believe that the plane may have exploded.

Lawrence Kusche claims that a crewman sneaking a cigarette could have been responsible for a spark that caused an explosion. Echoing Adams, Kusche says the Mariner aircraft were "flying gas tanks." But Michael J. Cusack, who flew planes of this type as an air force radio operator, does not accept that explanation. "I never heard of the planes being called 'flying gas tanks'. . . [and] it seems extremely unlikely that a crew member would sneak a cigarette during a rescue mission."

If no explosion occurred, then perhaps there was a collision at sea. Francis S. Gibson, a lieutenant aboard the steamship *Raleigh*, thought this might have happened to the *Cyclops*. He believed the ship "must have hit something at the wrong angle" and gone down. He says the ship could have gone down in ten seconds. Maybe this happened. But what could a ship almost as long as two football fields have collided with in midocean to cause it to sink before an SOS could be sent? If the obstacle had been another ship, the second vessel would be missing or damaged, too. Yet only the *Cyclops* was reported lost in that area at that time.

Collision seems a more likely cause when a *small* boat is missing. This may have been the case with the *Spray*.

A Skilled Sailor

When Joshua Slocum vanished in his thirty-six-foot sailboat, the world noticed. Slocum had won fame in 1898 when he became the first person to sail around the world alone. No one expected him to be lost at sea. He was an experienced sailor, who had, as the story goes, outraced pirates near Morocco, survived storms that destroyed larger ships nearby, and been stranded for a week in the Sargasso Sea, only to arrive home safely. Compared to these adventures, the trip he planned in 1909, from Rhode Island to Jamaica, should have been an easy one.

"When a vessel the size of a steamer or a tanker goes down, many objects usually float free, and a telltale oil slick bubbles to the surface sometimes for years to mark the spot where the ship sank. Yet in the Bermuda Triangle such evidence has never appeared."

Robert F. Burgess, *Sinkings, Salvages, and Shipwrecks*

"Experts point out that the swift current of the Gulf Stream quickly carries debris far from an accident site; 'lost without a trace' thus becomes easily understandable."

"Bermuda Triangle, Facts and Fiction," *Newsweek*, July 18, 1983

World sailor Capt. Joshua Slocum gave th s advice before disappearing in the Bermuda Triangle: "To young men contemplating a voyage, I would say go. The tales of rough usage are for the most part exaggerations, as also are the stories of sea danger."

Slocum inspected his boat, the *Spray*, on November 14, the day that was the start of his last voyage. He declared the yacht, in which he had circumnavigated the globe, completely seaworthy.

Yet Joshua Slocum and the *Spray* glided out into a calm sea and sailed away, never to be seen again. Some fellow sailors said the boat was not as seaworthy as Slocum claimed. One seaman who saw the boat just before it sailed said that it showed signs of wear and poor maintenance. He felt the boat had aged along with its master. If Slocum had died a natural death, the boat might have deteriorated to the point of sinking, with the body still aboard.

Slocum's son Victor disagreed. He said his father was in the best of health. Victor could think of only one possible solution to the mystery: the *Spray* must have been run down at night by an ocean liner.

No, said Captain Slocum's cronies, that was not likely. They had given him a strong and reliable beacon light to shine on his sails to avoid this very possibility.

Another suggestion was that Joshua Slocum, for an unknown reason, had wanted to escape his pres-

If the *Spray* was indeed seaworthy and its captain an expert sailor, what caused its disappearance?

ent life. Could he have sailed the *Spray* to some deserted island, where he lived out the rest of his days in solitude?

Some people think something like this could have happened to the *Cyclops* as well. Perhaps Captain Worley took the *Cyclops* to a place known only to him, where he and his crew lived out their lives, hidden away from the world. It seems unlikely that such a large ship could remain in hiding forever—or that the crew would have agreed to this plan, for Captain Worley was not a popular leader.

Richard Winer says the *Cyclops* was known as a "hell ship." He describes some of Worley's punishments for men who disobeyed his rules. As all the ship's company watched, Worley ordered the accused to remove their shoes and stockings. "Then at pistol point Worley drove the barefoot men around the ship's sun-scorched decks." After circling the ship, the men being disciplined were allowed to wash down their feet with seawater. Such punishments, combined with Worley's habit of walking the bridge dressed in nothing but long underwear and a derby hat, caused some of his crew to say he was crazy—and unfit for duty. Few would have been surprised if the crew aboard the *Cyclops* had planned to mutiny and take command of the ship themselves.

A May 1934 article in *Scientific American* quotes a navy informant, Will Talsey, who believed a mutiny may indeed have caused the disappearance of the huge vessel. However, Talsey thought those who conspired were not members of the crew.

Murderous Mutineers

When the *Cyclops* left the West Indies, says Talsey, it was carrying not only manganese ore, but a group of prisoners. Talsey describes them as "tough hombres . . . former convicts, thugs, burglars, and crooks of all kinds." Some of them had tried to murder the officers of another ship, the

"This relatively limited area is the scene of disappearances that total far beyond the laws of chance."

Vincent H. Gaddis, *Invisible Horizons*

"The triangle is no more prone to disappearances than other busy ocean regions."

"A Deadly Triangle," *Time*, January 6, 1975

Pittsburgh. They had been caught, arrested, and placed aboard the *Cyclops* for shipment home. All they had had to look forward to was prison—or death.

These men might have overpowered their guard and begun to sink the ship, with the idea of escaping in boats. These plans, Talsey says, could have gone awry if, for example, the heavily laden ship had sunk "too rapidly for the mutineers to swing the boats over the side and escape."

Or, Talsey surmises, maybe some of the desperados did get away in a boat. "Maybe they landed on the beach of one of the . . . villages that dot the Caribbean. Yes, maybe some are even there today. . . ."

Suppose mutineers did not sink the ship, but only *captured* it. Where could it go? Although a relatively small vessel can be repainted, renamed, and changed in other ways, the *Cyclops* was too big to disguise. It would have been conspicuous in any port, no matter how remote. Mutiny must be considered, however, when smaller craft seem to disappear into thin air. So must hijacking.

Hijacking

Pirates have always been a concern of seafarers. Sailors on watch keep one eye out for threatening ships, which could capture a vessel, put the captain and crew in irons, and sell the cargo for their own profit. No one seriously considered this as a possible cause of the disappearance of the *Cyclops* because its cargo was not one that could be easily resold.

However, in an article in the November 1974 issue of *Boating* magazine, Jim Martenhoff suggests that piracy is a real danger for boats at any time. Martenhoff quotes the claim of Congressman John Murphy that hundreds of yachts and small boats have been seized by dope smugglers: "These 20th Century pirates killed their captives, used the boats to smuggle drugs for two or three trips, then sank them at sea," said Murphy. Privately owned yachts and fishing boats are easy prey for smugglers and for people desperate to enter the United States. These boats often have no fixed schedules, and they can remain at sea for weeks without being missed by anyone.

Vacationers who practice bareboat chartering (renting a boat and sailing it themselves) are warned by the charter agencies to sail only in areas considered safe from hijacking. Dangerous areas are marked on the charts.

Yet the U.S. Coast Guard responded to Jim Martenhoff's article by saying it knew of only three cases of hijacking in more than thirty instances of vanished yachts in a three-year period. The Coast Guard calls the area known as the Bermuda Triangle the "most densely populated boating area in the

As the most densely populated boating area in the world, the Bermuda Triangle is a prime location for boating accidents.

Inexperienced pilots often have little practical knowledge of how to fly in certain weather conditions. Pilot error may be the cause of many of the disappearances of small planes.

world," and for that reason more accidents are bound to happen there. Most accidents, the Coast Guard says, are caused by human carelessness combined with extreme weather conditions.

A Lack of Seamanship Skills

People make errors, and those who vacation on the Caribbean islands east of Florida may have insufficient knowledge of the area's hazards. They are careless about checking weather reports, and they may lack seamanship skills. "All too often," says the Coast Guard, "crossings [of the Gulf Stream] are attempted with too small a boat." The current can take a boat far off its course in a very short time. When a captain in trouble gives the Coast Guard his or her position, the craft is often found "forty or fifty miles from where [the people] think they are."

Some vacationing crews do not know how to read a navigational chart. They may not even have one in their possession. In the 1988 video "The Case of the Bermuda Triangle," a Coast Guard spokesperson recounts a typical call received at his station:

"Where is [the island of] Bimini? It's not on our chart."

"What chart are you using?"

"I have the dictionary open to the World Atlas."

Competent sailors know that it is necessary to consult up-to-date navigational charts when setting a course. Hundreds of islands in the Bahamas look alike, and the same is true of the islands in the West Indies. Pleasure seekers can get hopelessly lost, especially if they view their trip as a party. Intoxicated boat operators are as much a hazard on the sea as drunk drivers are on the highways.

Pilot Error

Private planes run into difficulty, too. A pilot may have little knowledge of how to fly in fog or may become disoriented when water and sky seem to blend into one. Again, as with boaters, a flier may lack navigational skills. Athley Gamber, widow of a pilot who disappeared in a flight between Florida and the Bahamas, believes that "pilot error is responsible for fifty percent of the disappearances of small private planes." Undoubtedly, she says, perhaps 25 percent have simply run out of gas.

But the pilots of commercial, passenger, and military planes constantly check the weather, their instruments, and certainly their gas gauges. Ignorance seems a less likely reason for their disappearances.

Pilots have been known to have heart attacks while flying, and entire crews of boats have become ill from food poisoning, since food spoils easily in the tropics. Yet these causes cannot account for all

"The mysterious menace that haunts the Atlantic off the Florida coast . . . strikes again and again—swallowing a ship or a plane, or leaving behind a derelict with no life aboard."

Vincent A. Gaddis, *Invisible Horizons*

"Admittedly, by any name it is a part of the world to approach with caution, although the reasons are natural, rather than supernatural."

Writer Carleton Mitchell, *Boating* magazine, October 1984

the ships and planes, large and small, that have met their doom in this triangle of mystery. Perhaps most mysterious of all is that in so many of the puzzling Bermuda Triangle disappearances, not a scrap of wreckage is known to have washed ashore *anywhere*.

Not a Trace

Well-known treasure salvager Mel Fisher, offers some possible reasons for this. For one thing, wreckage that sank could be covered with shifting sand or quicksand. Fisher observes that quicksands in the Bermuda Triangle "have been noted to swallow fairly large boats which became stuck in the sandy bottom."

Could a gigantic area of quicksand have swallowed the *Cyclops*, its prisoners, and all its crew? It is a chilling possibility. Divers have tried repeatedly over the years to find the vessel's hull, or at least some trace of it, on the ocean floor. They have come up empty-handed.

Almost as eerie as quicksand is the idea of a boat being lost in an undersea cavern. The ocean floor is not a vast, level plain of sand. In Bahamian waters can be found limestone formations pitted by huge, cavelike holes. The water in these holes is a remarkable light blue. Chambers and passageways branch off among the caves, some to a depth of fifteen hundred feet. Dangerously strong currents sweep through the caves. In a January 1993 article in *Fate* magazine, writer John Miller recalls that, in 1983, Jacques Cousteau photographed "a perfectly preserved, turn-of-the-century rowboat sitting on a shelf about eighty feet down, as though carefully placed there by some mermaid who collected antique vessels." Small craft have been found at lesser levels, too.

If divers were to search deep inside these passages, perhaps more small boats, skeletons of ancient mariners, and bits of wreckage could be found.

"It was as if some mysterious sea monster, like the kraken so feared by mariners centuries ago, had swallowed the vessel whole."

Writer Jim Martenhoff, *Boating*, November 1974

"There has never been a documented case on file of an octopus or eel ever attacking a boat or ship, or for that matter a person, other than in self defense."

Author John Wallace Spencer, *No Earthly Explanation*

A diver explores a blue hole. Some theories suggest that wreckage of lost vessels can be found in these unexplored undersea caverns.

So far, all the theories explored have been based on scientific knowledge, logical possibilities, and the experience of people familiar with the area known as the Bermuda Triangle. However, other theories have been suggested, theories that are more speculation than fact. Some students of the problem ask, What if there's a living creature out there, something that spends most of its time far beneath the surface of the sea?

Frank W. Lane, in his book *Nature Parade*, reports that giant squid have been found: "In one specimen the tentacles measured thirty-seven feet, and it is possible that there exist in the deep oceans squids spanning one hundred feet."

Engulfed by Giant Squids

The *Literary Digest* for March 8, 1919, explored the idea of a sea creature pulling the *Cyclops* down to the depths of the sea. The magazine recalled tales of ships "suddenly engulfed by colossal cuttle-fishes" (giant squids). In one of these stories, three men were standing on planks slung over the side of a vessel, "when an enormous cuttlefish rose from the water and . . . tore away the scaffolding on which they stood." Two of the men were lost, but

Were the *Cyclops* and its crew victims of a legendary sea creature?

Throughout history, sailors have recounted tales of strange and eerie creatures of the sea.

the third hung tightly to the rigging and screamed for help. "His shipmates ran to his assistance and succeeded in rescuing him by cutting away the creature's arms with axes and knives, but he died delirious on the following night." One of the cut-off arms was said to be twenty-five feet long and "to have had on it suckers as big as sauce-pan lids."

Such stories are interesting to hear, but Richard Winer does not think that any such creature was responsible for the loss of the *Cyclops*. Winer does, however, recount an incident in which he himself saw something "phenomenal" off the coast of Bermuda.

A giant sea serpent overpowers a sailing vessel.

The thing Winer saw was "maybe 150 feet across." It was deep purple and moved slowly up from the ocean's depth. The movement was similar to that of pulsating jellyfish, which normally measure six inches in diameter. Winer said he watched "awestricken" until the strange creature sank slowly into the blackening ocean. Winer ruled out the suggestion that it was a giant squid. Instead he wondered whether he had seen a monstrous jellyfish.

Eaten by Sea Monsters

Sea monsters, if they exist, may account for the ships that are found afloat with only the people missing. George Noble offers this suggestion, quoted in the 1919 *Literary Digest* article:

> About the only possible explanation . . . is that Gargantuan Squids . . . may have helped themselves to the ship's people as delicately and effectually as one plucks gooseberries off a bush—then sunk out of sight and left scarcely a ripple behind.

It sounds like science fiction, but Anton Bruun, a Danish oceanographer, captured something that convinced him that giant creatures might live in the sea under the Bermuda Triangle. In 1930 Bruun wrote:

> I have never seen a Giant Sea Serpent but I have a very good reason to believe that such a creature exists. I saw an eel-like fish in tadpole stage six feet long, while a young zoologist aboard a trawler off West Africa. There was a larval form of the eel in our nets. It was typical in all respects except size. It could be expected to grow to 72 feet. We weren't lucky enough to find his parents. I have searched for them for twenty years.

Only a whale is bigger than this eel would have become.

It is known that European eels migrate to the Sargasso Sea to breed, following an ancient undersea "river" of ocean currents. Were giant eels the creatures old-time sailors claimed to have seen swimming among the weeds?

Could the *Cyclops* have been pulled to the bottom of the sea by a giant monster of the deep? "Many supposed clues to the loss have appeared over the years, but none were authentic," writes Lawrence Kusche. The *Cyclops* "was the first large radio-equipped ship to disappear without sending an SOS and it was the largest Navy ship ever to be lost without a trace. . . . Its loss continues to be rightfully called the 'most baffling mystery in the annals of the Navy.'"

"I would like to point out that after years of research into this matter—I have yet to come across a clear-cut case of piracy without evidence of violence, the transfer of cargo and valuables, or deliberate wrecking. It is this that makes these cases of disappearances of people from sound ships so mysterious and puzzling."

Ivan T. Sanderson, *Invisible Residents*

"Modern-day pirates are known to exist but on a limited scale, attacking small boats with crews of one or two."

John Wallace Spencer, *Limbo of the Lost—Today*

Five

Other Times, Other Places

(Opposite page) Why do
planes mysteriously vanish in
the Bermuda Triangle?
Scientists are investigating
theories that time warps or
supernatural forces are
responsible for the
disappearances.

Many attempts have been made to solve the mystery of the Bermuda Triangle disappearances. Some of the suggestions could have come straight out of science fiction. For instance, some experts have suggested that strange aberrations in time are the cause. The possibility of time travel has fascinated writers and scientists alike for many decades. Science fiction authors often drop characters into the past or propel them into the future, triggering strange and interesting events. This literary device is called a time warp. Webster's dictionary defines it as "the condition or process of being displaced from one point in time to another, as in science fiction." If time warps exist, they are wrinkles in the otherwise smooth flow of time, and they could be the cause of some strange incidents.

Another intriguing possibility is that forces from other worlds may suck people and vessels into places beyond our knowledge. Some of these places may be below the sea. Others may be far above it. In his novel *Twenty Thousand Leagues Under the Sea*, Jules Verne used his imagination to explore the first possibility. Television shows such as *Star Trek* have used make-believe settings, fictional characters, and an incredibly advanced technology to tell

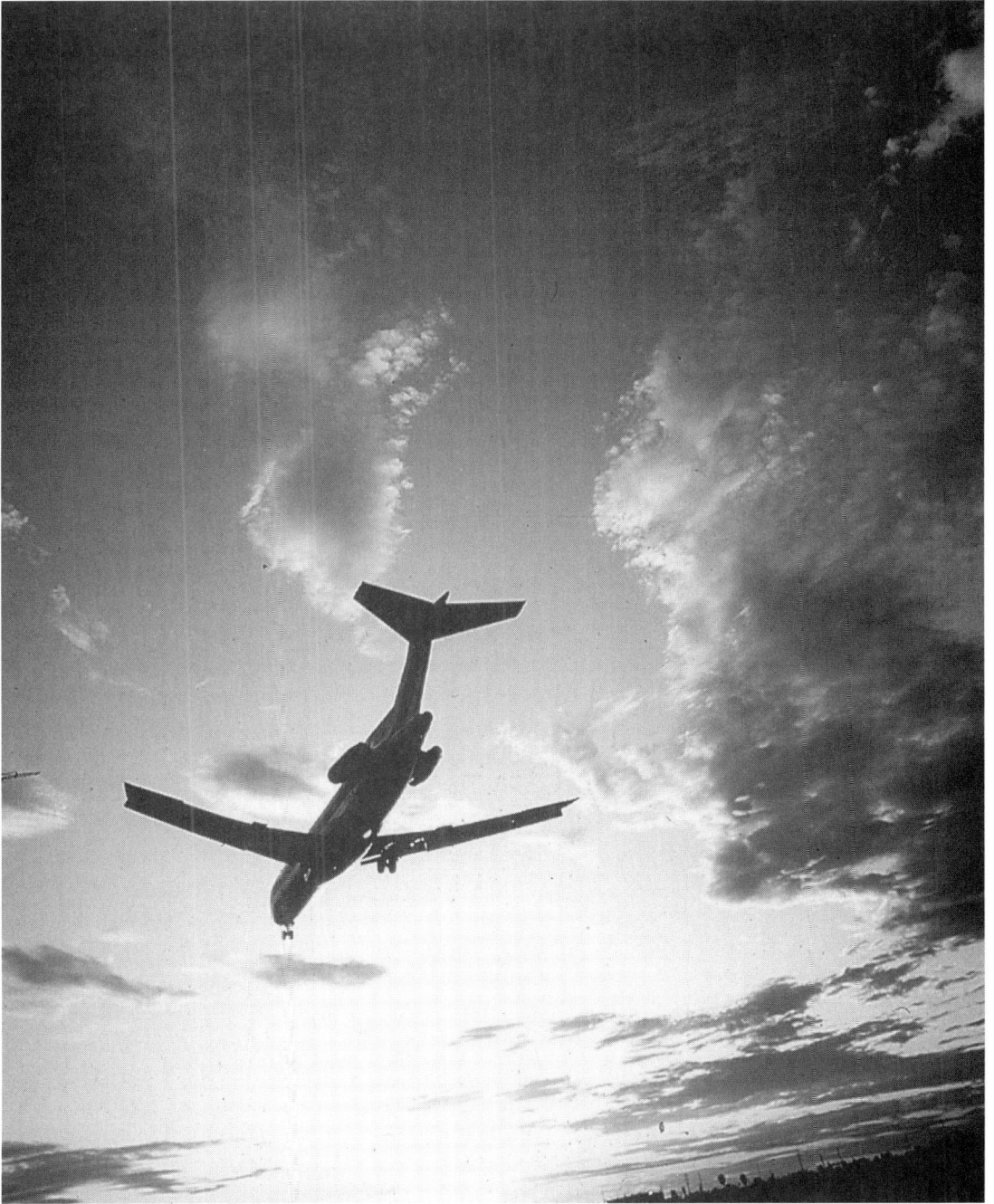

stories about what humans might encounter if they were whisked to places beyond the earth.

Time Warps

Scientists are investigating theories such as these. One day scientists may learn whether they are reality or merely fiction. Their findings may explain what happened to people like pilot Bruce Gernon, who had an extraordinary experience in his light plane during a flight from the Bahamas to Florida in 1970. But until then, no one, not even Gernon himself, may be able to explain that day's mysterious events.

Edward F. Dolan Jr. describes Gernon's flight: "A great cloud loomed in front of [the pilot] soon after takeoff. He flew above it, only to have it chase him." Then it closed around him. Gernon said the cloud was shaped like a tunnel. Some of his instruments stopped working.

According to Dolan, "Gernon flew along inside the cloud for several minutes. At last, he broke free."

Gernon arrived at his destination a half hour earlier than normal flight time for the trip. His plane *could not* have flown that fast. Yet it had.

In discussing early arrival cases such as Gernon's, Charles Berlitz says, "The only possible [natural] explanation would be that they had a tail wind behind them blowing, for example, at 500 miles per hour," and that is a most unlikely possibility. Ivan T. Sanderson points out that a wind that strong would be devastating to people on the ground. No such wind was reported during Gernon's flight.

Sanderson's explanation for such happenings is that "the planes ran into a local *time* anomaly [irregularity] rather than into incredible, undetected, and seemingly impossible winds." Did Gernon then fly into a place where time does not flow at a regular rate? We do not know. If it did happen, however, it would appear that Gernon got out of this time warp.

Others may not have been so lucky.

Norman Slater is noted for his extraordinary sensitivity to physical forces. He is said to have extrasensory perception—that is, to be able to perceive, or see, matters beyond the range of ordinary senses. Slater believes that people and objects who have disappeared are held in a sort of time funnel and that there are such time funnels in the Bermuda Triangle. He claims that objects lost in them are preserved, but people are not. Objects, such as ships and planes, might eventually be released from the funnel, later to be found mysteriously empty of life. On the other hand, people who get out of the time funnel would be skeletons, if anything remained at all. Slater does not say what would have killed the people.

Some people automatically dismiss so-called psychic experiences such as Slater's. But scientists

Pilot Bruce Gerron reports having flown through a mysterious tunnel-shaped cloud that may have looked like this.

no longer ignore completely these paranormal phenomena. Research has shown that there *are* people who have unusual abilities to "know" things the rest of us do not perceive.

Scientific investigator Stanley Krippner says many scientists themselves have had paranormal experiences. They do not consider them silly or merely amusing. After much study and many well-controlled experiments, Krippner has come to the conclusion that there are places in the world where "living things and objects do not behave as they ordinarily would." In an article by Paul Chance in the October 1973 issue of *Psychology Today*, Krippner states: "Some physicists are talking about particles that are unstable in time and space; this brings up the possibility that there are different time universes with which we could interact."

Some of the more than one hundred ships and planes that have vanished in the deadly waters of the Bermuda Triangle.

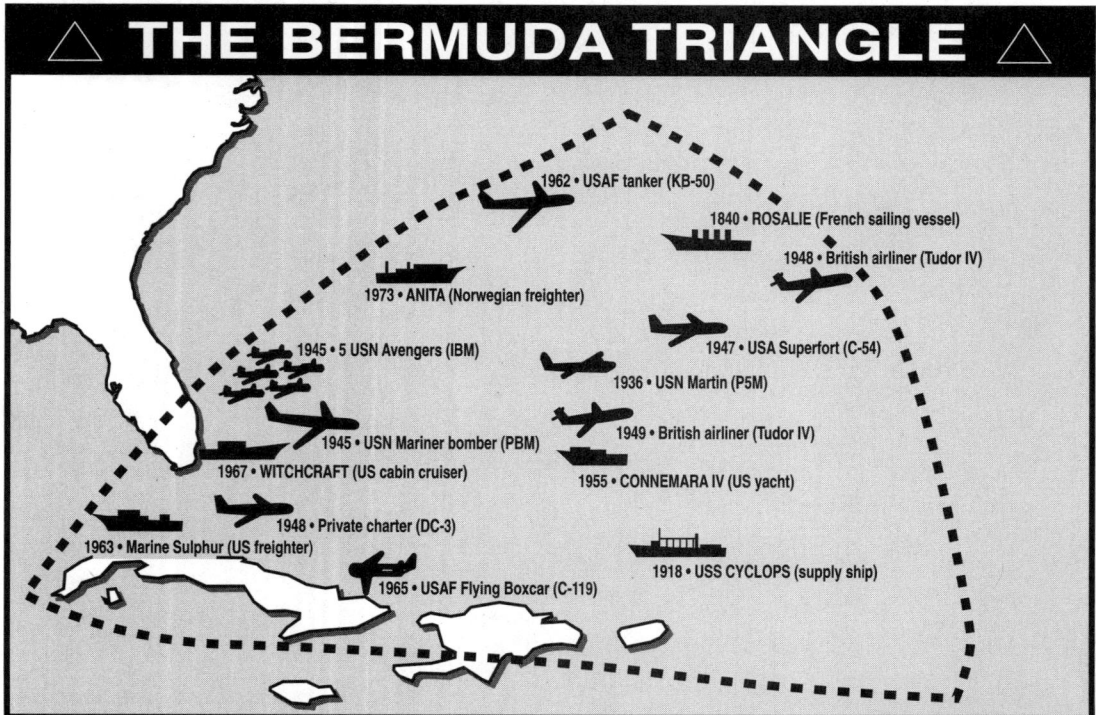

△ THE BERMUDA TRIANGLE △

1962 • USAF tanker (KB-50)

1840 • ROSALIE (French sailing vessel)

1948 • British airliner (Tudor IV)

1973 • ANITA (Norwegian freighter)

1945 • 5 USN Avengers (IBM)

1947 • USA Superfort (C-54)

1936 • USN Martin (P5M)

1945 • USN Mariner bomber (PBM)

1949 • British airliner (Tudor IV)

1967 • WITCHCRAFT (US cabin cruiser)

1955 • CONNEMARA IV (US yacht)

1948 • Private charter (DC-3)

1963 • Marine Sulphur (US freighter)

1918 • USS CYCLOPS (supply ship)

1965 • USAF Flying Boxcar (C-119)

The idea that people can travel through, around, into, and out of time sounds fantastic. Yet world-famous scientist Albert Einstein theorized that height, width, and depth are not the only dimensions to be considered in scientific calculations. He said that time, the fourth dimension, must be included also.

Time Eddies

Lawrence Kusche says that as the Bermuda Triangle legend is usually told, time does not always move in a straight line—"parts of it occasionally break off and head away from the main flow, carrying with them whatever might happen to be in the area." Such a time eddy would be much like the whirling ocean currents called eddies. But instead of whisking debris away from a wreck, or a ship into the ocean depths, a time eddy—if in fact there were such a thing—could whirl ships off their normal course and into another dimension. These vessels and their unfortunate occupants might be trapped in a parallel universe.

Oceanographer Dr. J. Manson Valentine defines a parallel universe as a place very like our world but undetectable to us. Such a place would have a sun of its own, with planets and stars similar to those in earth's universe. According to this view, people from ships and planes caught in time anomalies could be living on a sister planet of earth. Valentine does not say what he thinks the people in this dimension are doing or whether they are able to live out a normal life span.

Berlitz calls this sort of whisking away a "magnetic tear in the curtain of time." He suggests that a combination of magnetic whirlpools and gravity may be causing time to behave in an unusual manner.

The facts in another strange case suggest that something of this sort may have happened to Carolyn Cascio, slowly sucking her aircraft away from its destination one day many years ago. On June 7,

"I have the strong feeling that these logical possibilities are not enough. Part of the puzzle is always missing."

Oceanographer Jim Thorne, in the preface to Spencer's *Limbo of the Lost—Today*

"Though we have done extensive research in this particular area for over 50 years, no unexplainable events have taken place. Our scientists give no credence to the mysteries reported to have occurred in this area."

Public information officer Nancy Green, Woods Hole Oceanographic Institution, letter to the author, March 3, 1986

Clairvoyant Edgar Cayce believed that a strange underwater force wreaked havoc on boats and planes in the Bermuda Triangle.

1964, Cascio left Nassau with one passenger, intending to land at Grand Turk Island, Bahamas. When her calculations showed she was over Grand Turk, however, she *could not see* the island. Cascio radioed fragmented comments. She reported, "Nothing is down there." Later she radioed, "Is there any way out of this?"

Observers on the ground saw a light plane presumed to be Cascio's circle the island for about half an hour before it disappeared. It was never seen again.

The people on the ground could not understand why Carolyn Cascio had not seen the island, since they had seen her. Did an unknown force pull the aircraft into another dimension? Are Cascio and her passenger living even now in a parallel universe?

Perhaps time, gravity, and magnetism have been factors in some of the disappearances. Perhaps not. No one yet knows how to explain why people appear to have been pulled into another dimension. People only speculate that such phenomena may exist. They also ask whether there could be some other force—or some other *place*—that pulls planes away from their destinations.

Under the Sea

Edgar Cayce believed that a strange force found in the ocean depths affected travelers in the Triangle area. Cayce was a clairvoyant, a person to whom information—often about future events—is revealed in a trance. After one of his deep, trancelike sleeps in 1940, Cayce predicted that underwater ruins would be "discovered under the slime of ages of seawater—near what is known as Bimini [in the Bahamas], off the coast of Florida." These ruins, according to Cayce, were a portion of the lost continent of Atlantis, which, Cayce predicted, would rise again at some future time.

The ancient Greek philosopher Plato described Atlantis as a powerful empire with "golden cities."

Its citizens built temples, walls, roads, and pyramids. About twelve thousand years ago, however, this civilization came to a sudden end. Some force, possibly an earthquake, a flood, or an immense volcanic explosion, caused this legendary land to sink into the sea.

Edgar Cayce said that when Atlantis sank, it took with it powerful crystals that had been developed into sources of destruction. In 1970, Ray Brown, a diver and lecturer, claimed to have found a mysterious crystal on one of his dives in the Bahamas. His find seems to support Cayce's revelation.

"I turned to look toward the sun through the murky water," says Brown, "and saw a pyramid shape shining like a mirror. About thirty-five to forty feet from the top was an opening. I was reluctant to

A seventeenth-century map shows a possible location of the mysterious lost continent of Atlantis.

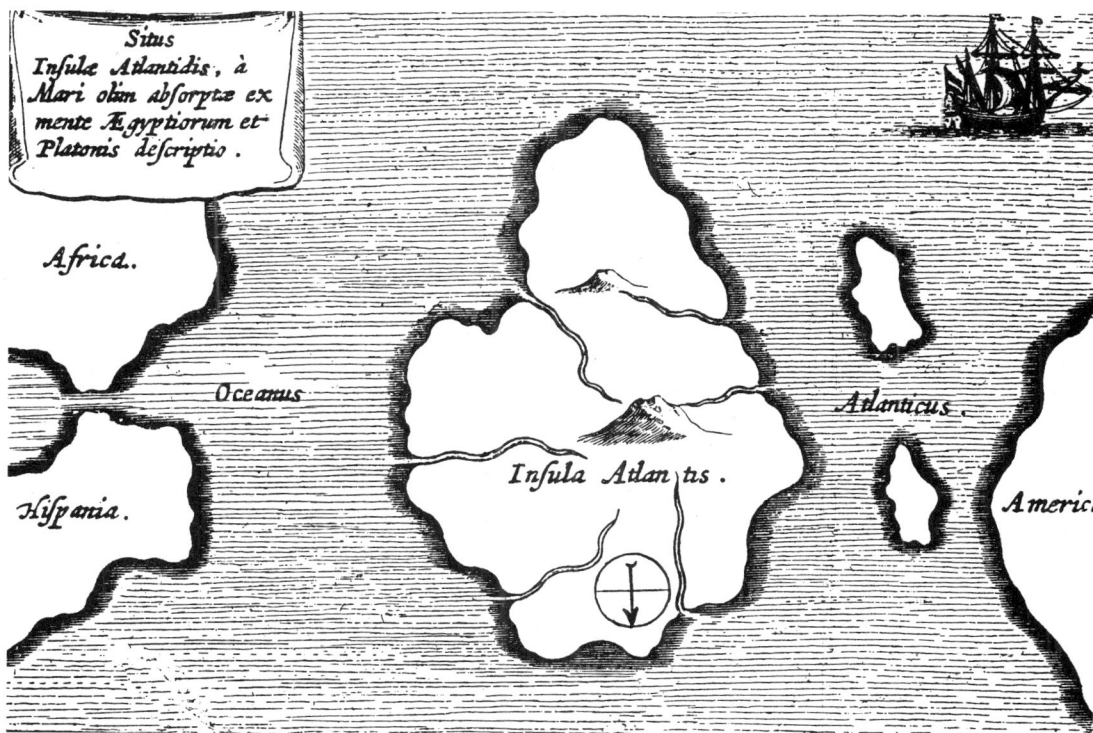

Situs Insulæ Atlantidis, à Mari olim abforptæ ex mente Ægyptiorum et Platonis defcriptio.

Africa.

Oceanus

Hifpania.

Insula Atlantis.

Atlanticus.

America.

go inside . . . but I swam in anyway." Then, Brown says, he saw a crystal, held by two metallic hands. He loosened it, and, "as soon as I grabbed it, I felt this was the time to get out and not come back."

Brown still has the crystal, which he shows to lecture audiences. According to Charles Berlitz, this small crystal seems to cause a throbbing sensation in the hands of those who hold it.

Whether huge underwater crystals, if they exist, are powerful enough to affect ships and planes in the Bermuda Triangle is difficult to prove. In any event, the existence of Atlantis has never been proved, and archaeologist Marshall McKusick thinks that Cayce's method of psychically digging out information from the past was highly unreliable. He says that Cayce had an overheated imagination and that his theories were based on "phony revelations about antiquity."

The writers of Funk and Wagnalls Encyclopedia, though, believe there may be some basis for belief in Atlantis. They say "the possibility exists that [Plato] had access to records no longer extant [in existence]."

Maybe what is under the sea has nothing to do with Atlantis. Maybe it has nothing to do with crystals. But the author of *Great Mysteries of the Air* thinks *something* there may be changing gravity, magnetism, and electronic systems. Ralph Barker claims there is evidence that "matter completely contrary to that known on this planet . . . may be embedded in localized areas of the earth." This matter, says Barker, may have arrived from outer space.

Unidentified Flying Objects

Scientists and writers have explored the possibility that UFOs may have something to do with disappearances in the Bermuda Triangle. Perhaps these UFOs, or flying saucers, deposited something in the sea. Could they have dropped a device that causes compasses to spin, radios to die, and ships to

"[Researchers] found its sea floor covered with all sorts of astonishing things, including dust from outer space which had fallen upon earth and sunk into the sea."

Author Alan Villiers, *The Wild Ocean*

"Little green men with red-rimmed eyes emerge only in saloons after midnight."

Author Clive Cussler, *Ladies' Home Journal*, January 1978

Do UFOs have something to do with the disappearances in the Bermuda Triangle?

sink? Flying saucer sightings occur all over the world, but according to Elwood D. Baumann, author of *The Devil's Triangle*, more of these reports come from the Bermuda Triangle than anywhere else. Why might this be?

Baumann is not the only writer who sees a connection between UFOs and the Triangle. John Godwin, in his book *This Baffling World*, says, "A curious thing about saucer sightings is that they seem to come in batches." He speculates that they may appear only when conditions are right for them to have an easy flight. Perhaps conditions are right more often in the Bermuda Triangle than in other places on earth.

Some people do not believe flying saucers exist. But writer Jim Martenhoff relates an experience in the Bermuda Triangle that made a believer out of him. In his article in the November 1974 issue of *Boating* magazine, Martenhoff tells how he and some friends were returning from a lonely spot "in an empty sea" off the east coast of Florida. Suddenly their engine blew. The boat began filling with water, and they hastily hooked up pumps. After working furiously, Martenhoff says, he and his friends "dumped 10,000 gallons of water back in the ocean where it belonged." They thought the danger was over.

Then, thirty minutes later, two strange objects drifted through the air, across the ship's bow. They came in straight and low over the water. "At the last minute, they turned away," says Bob Lewis, captain of the fishing vessel on which the men were sailing. Martenhoff reports, "The objects remained in sight for almost two minutes—long enough for us to focus our binoculars and study them with care. They were hazy white against a clear blue sky. . . . They seemed to be quite large and quite far away." Martenhoff and his friends were convinced that the objects were not airplanes or helicopters. Instead they were "like inverted bowls flattened on the bottom. . . . We saw stubby, wing-like projections jutting out from their sides."

When the objects picked up speed and disappeared, Martenhoff wondered whether he and his friends had narrowly missed becoming another boat and crew lost without a trace in the Bermuda Triangle. "We simply have no logical explanation for what we saw," concluded Martenhoff.

Alien Visits

No logical explanation has been found, either, for the four ghost vessels sighted within fourteen days off the coast of Bermuda in 1969. Author John Wallace Spencer reports that the ships were found a few days apart—and all their crews were missing. The London Weather Center reported that there had been "no gale force conditions which could account for them."

If no natural explanation can be advanced for the disappearance of the crews on these ships, then what—or who—is responsible?

After studying these four cases, Spencer concluded that extraterrestrial beings on board UFOs had been responsible. If this extraordinary claim were found to be true, however, the question of motive would remain. *Why* would aliens remove seemingly average people from seemingly average vessels?

Dr. Carl Sagan, director of the Laboratory for Planetary Studies at Cornell University, has written a book called *Intelligent Life in the Universe*, in which he speculates on what representatives of an extraterrestrial civilization might want of us. "We would not be useful as slaves," he says, since a society capable of spaceflight would have adequate machines as servants. "They could not want us for food," Sagan continues, "since such an advanced society should be able to make its own food." He says we cannot rule out the possibility that they may want to convert us to their religion. Or they may want to crush us so they will remain the superior power in the universe.

Curious Visitors

John Godwin, who entertains the possibility that such visitors exist, theorizes that they come out of curiosity—perhaps to acquire specimens for a kind of space zoo.

J. Manson Valentine suggests that extraterrestrials may be studying us, much as we study people of different cultures and different historical periods. Perhaps extraterrestrials are concerned that as we progress technically, we may do something to destroy our planet, an act that could in some way

Scientists such as Carl Sagan speculate on why aliens would want to abduct humans.

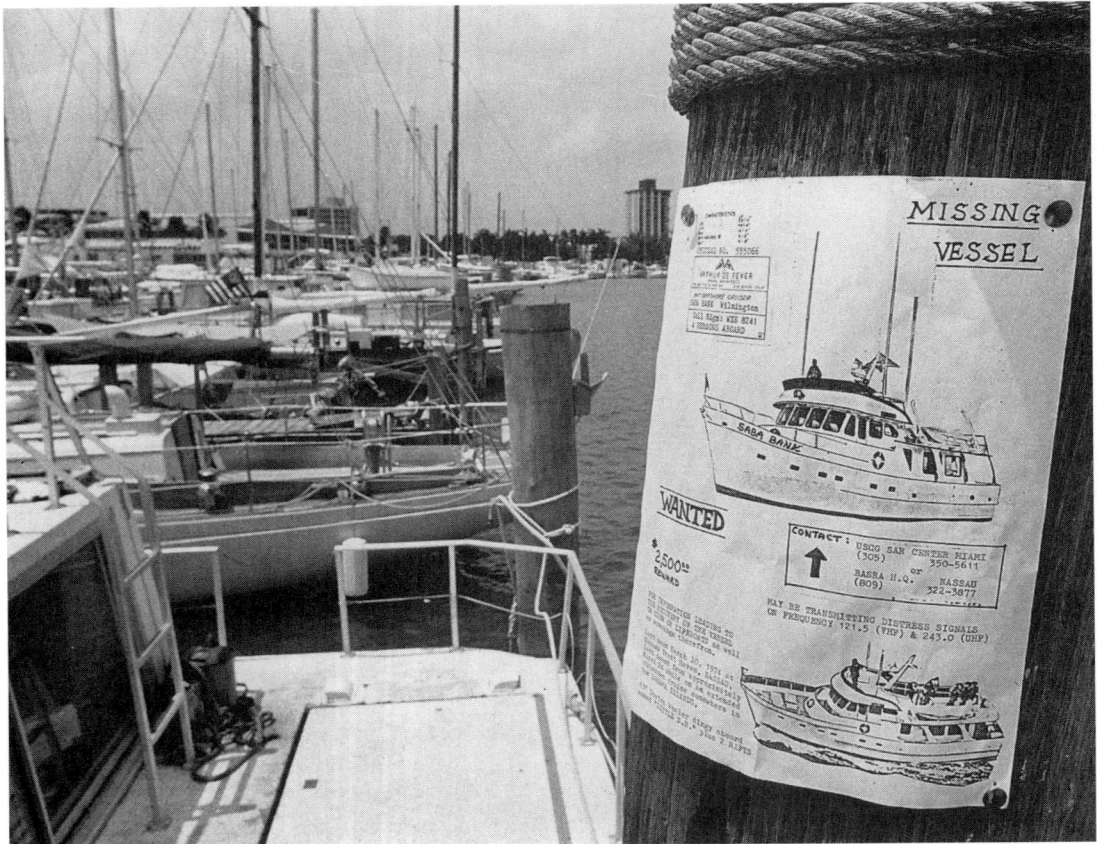

A poster offers a $2,500 reward for information leading to the recovery of a vessel and its crew lost in the Bermuda Triagle.

affect their own environment. Have they come to save us—and themselves as well?

UFOs Underwater

George Johnson and Don Tanner do not think the beings on UFOs are so kind. In their book *The Bible and the Bermuda Triangle*, Johnson and Tanner say the creatures on UFOs are "evil entities." These demons, or devils, are taking human spirits down into a "nether world," an underground place where people's souls go when they die. These authors claim there is more than one entrance to this nether world, more commonly known as Hell. They cite the Bible as the source of their belief. The gates of Hell are mentioned in the Gospel of Matthew (16:18), and Johnson and Tanner believe the demons take people through one of these gates. They think it is possible that because of the mysterious disappearances in the Bermuda Triangle, some of the gates of Hell may be located there.

Spencer, too, thinks something evil may be happening beneath the Triangle. He believes extraterrestrial beings have built bases and laboratory facilities deep under the ocean.

> I believe they chose this particular area because it's the most heavily traveled in the world. If my theory is correct, extraterrestrial scientists are conducting continuous experiments with earth beings and their machinery. . . . Whenever they want or need someone or something for experimental purposes, all they have to do is leave their facilities, take what they want, and return to their hidden underwater laboratories.

Stories such as one told by Betty and Barney Hill seem to support Spencer's theory that extraterrestrials abduct humans for experiments or merely

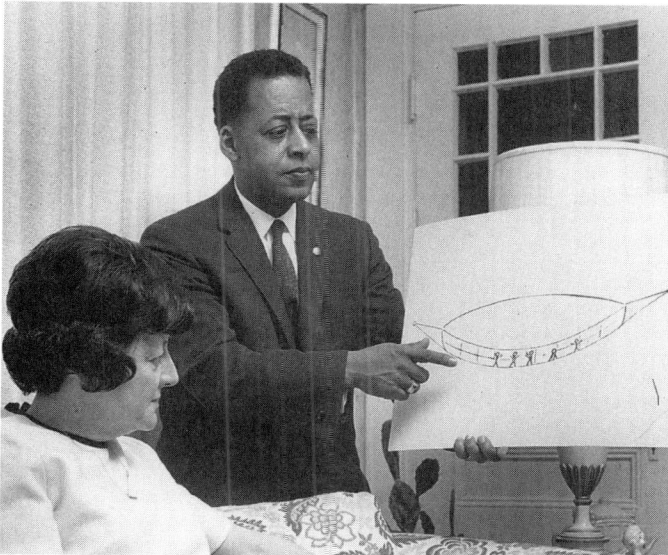

Betty and Barney Hill describe the spaceship they say abducted them.

for study. The Hills said that as they drove down a highway in New Hampshire on September 19, 1961, they encountered a UFO in the sky above their car. They became drowsy, and when they awoke, two hours had passed. Later, under hypnosis, they recalled that they had undergone medical examinations conducted by slender uniformed humanoids with large slanted eyes, bald heads, no noses, and slitlike mouths. The Hills' experience—if it is more than a fantasy—represents what Spencer has in mind.

Military Involvement

During World War II bomber pilots over Germany and Japan reported that strange objects sometimes flew alongside or behind their aircraft. They described the objects as fiery balls of light or as glowing disks. At first the pilots were alarmed, but it soon became obvious that the mysterious objects were not dangerous.

During World War II, U.S. bomber pilots reported seeing glowing objects zooming alongside their aircraft. These strange but harmless objects were never explained.

In January 1948, the U.S. Air Force formed a secret group to study and evaluate information concerning sightings and phenomena in the atmosphere. The group, called Project Sign, concluded that UFOs were from other planets. Not everyone in the military accepted this conclusion. Later, the air force adopted a policy of attributing the sightings to normal occurrences in the atmosphere, such as movements of clouds, stars, or meteors.

As more people reported unusual sightings in the sky, the military worried that UFOs might be a threat to national security. Consequently the air force reorganized its program. The new program was called Project Bluebook. From 1952 to 1969, the air force analyzed 12,618 sightings from all over the United States. "The vast majority proved to have simple explanations," reports Richard Michael Rasmussen in his book, *Extraterrestrial Life*. Some of the objects were weather balloons, some were meteors, some only strangely shaped clouds. Some were hoaxes—stories made up to get attention for the storyteller.

Project Bluebook closed down in 1969 when the air force decided it could no longer be justified on the ground of national security or in the interest of science. However, 718 objects remain unidentified. The air force had no explanation for their existence.

Sightings continue to occur and interested scientists continue to study UFOs. When they discover what UFOs are, some of the Bermuda Triangle disappearances may be explained also.

Six

The Mystery Remains

Forty-six years after their disappearance, the five planes of Flight 19 again made news. On May 27, 1991, both *Newsweek* and *Time* magazines announced that the lost patrol might have been found, just ten miles off the east coast of Florida. In its June 3, 1991, issue, *People* magazine devoted four pages to a story entitled "The Sea Yields Its Lost Squadron." A subheading suggested: "The undersea discovery of five World War II planes may solve the Bermuda Triangle mystery."

People's story, illustrated with photos of the missing airmen, begins:

> The sonar images flashed a garish blue in the control room of the *Deep See* as it slipped through the dark waters off the coast of Fort Lauderdale, Florida. For the crew of the 60-foot research-and-exploration vessel, the night of May 8 started routinely enough as they scanned the ocean floor in search of sunken galleons or anything else salvageable.

In the early morning hours, something intriguing appeared on the screen—a computer-generated outline of an airplane lying on the bottom of the sea 750 feet below. The crew lowered their underwater camera and stared at the image of a Navy Avenger.

(Opposite page) Dick Adams, who worked on the rescue mission for Flight 19 nearly half a century ago, still searches for answers to the mystery.

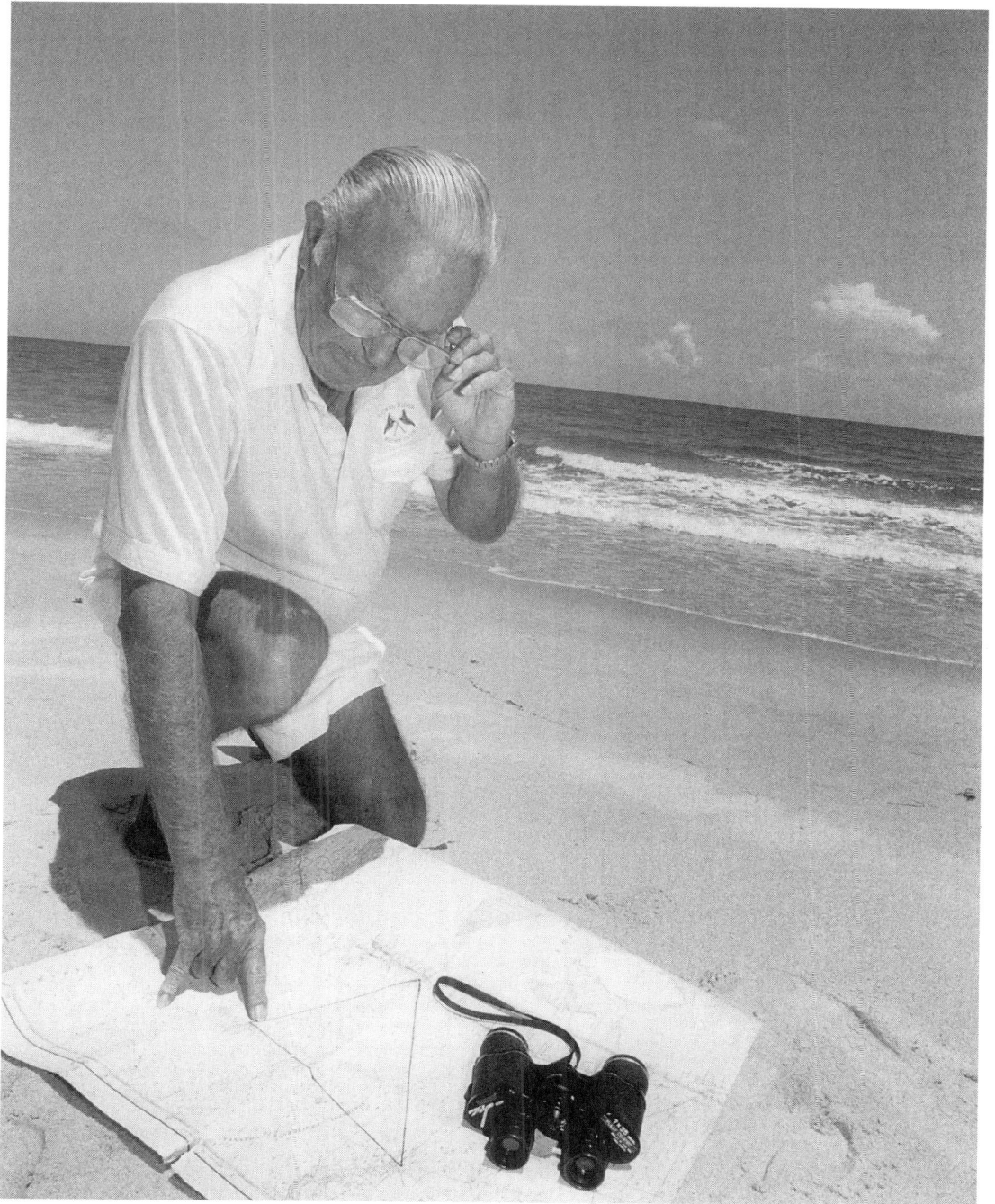

The aircraft's wreckage had star roundels on the wings. Those and the distinctive rear gun turret marked it as the type of plane lost nearly a half-century ago.

Excitement mounted as the sonar picked up the image of another plane. Then a third. Over the next twenty-four hours, the salvage crew spotted five planes in all, lying within a one-mile radius. "We were pretty thrilled," said sonar operator Bill Mastrude. "We were all saying, 'Nobody's going to believe us at home.'"

The newly discovered aircraft appeared to have been ditched. The cabin canopies were open, and some of the propeller blades were bent back. One of the planes had the marking *FT* on its side—the designation for the Fort Lauderdale base. Another had a *28,* the number of flight leader Taylor's plane. The country waited for verification that Flight 19 had been found. A court battle over the rights to the wreckage began between the Scientific Search Project—the owners of the *Deep See*—and the U.S. Navy. Movie and television rights would be worth millions of dollars.

"Let Them Rest"

If the newly found wreckage turned out to be Flight 19, the crew would have been a pitifully short distance from safety when they perished. Susan Powers Spengler, daughter of crew member Edward Powers, told *People* magazine reporters that she would like to have the identities of the aircraft confirmed. If the remains of her father and the others were found, however, Spengler hoped they would not be disturbed: "I don't want them brought up. Let them be. Let them rest."

Finally, on June 17, 1991, *Time* followed up on the story. In "It's Still the Lost Squadron," their writers announced that "in a surprise about-face last week, high-tech salvagers who found [the Avengers] announced they were not the Lost Squadron after all.

"The five fully armed Avengers that took off . . . with their 14 crewmen and disappeared without a trace have inspired more rumors and theories than a forestful of Bigfoots."

Bill Hewitt et al., *People*, June 3, 1991

"Whatever it is, is still going on out there."

Charles Berlitz, telephone conversation with Norma Gaffron, March 1986

Capt. Keith Callcway (left) and submersible robot designer Graham Hawkes, shown here, were among the crew that discovered the wreckage of five airplanes off the coast of Florida.

They appeared to be five separate aircraft that had crashed within 1½ miles of each other on individual training missions." The announcement in *Time* kept the Bermuda Triangle mystery intact.

Still unanswered is the question of what caused the pilots of Flight 19 to lose their bearings. *People* magazine quoted the man who had been the flight training officer on that fateful day in 1945. Retired Lt. Comdr. Don Poole said he knew from Taylor's radio transmissions that the twenty-eight-year-old pilot "was only getting himself more confused. It can happen to a pilot when you look out and you don't see anything familiar." Poole, now living in Cape Coral, Florida, added, "Usually you snap out of that panic and stay on course. But he didn't."

Lawrence Kusche, in his book *The Disappearance of Flight 19*, says he thinks he knows what confused the squadron leader: "Taylor had just transferred to Fort Lauderdale from Miami, where he was used to flying in the Keys. In between the

Abacos [a group of islands in the Bahamas], if you look to the right, there are lots of islands that look like the Keys."

Perhaps whatever happened to Taylor and his crew—and the reasons for it—will never be known. Graham Hawkes, who headed the search in 1991, shrugs off the idea that Flight 19 was a victim of the Bermuda Triangle. "I don't know where Flight 19 is," he says, "but it's certainly in the ocean and not up with the aliens anywhere."

The story of Flight 19 is one of the cornerstones of the legend of the Bermuda Triangle. An unnamed writer for *Time* magazine believes the triangle to be a myth,

born on a slow news day in 1950. That's when an Associated Press reporter named E.V.W. Jones collated a report of various planes and ships lost off the Florida coast and put it on the wire. The story was picked up and enlarged by other news services, tabloids and magazines until the Bermuda Triangle . . . was a cultural fixation.

Sonar operator Bill Mastrude (right) and John Vance examine a high-resolution image of one of the sunken Navy Avengers.

Aircrew members pose in front of the torpedo bomber number 28, the lead plane from the "Lost Squadron." The search for definitive answers to the disappearance of Flight 19 and the other mysteries of the Bermuda Triangle continues.

Lawrence Kusche says, "No [one] theory so far proposed has been able to account satisfactorily for all or even most of the [Bermuda Triangle] incidents." But he believes that taken one at a time, logical explanations can be found for most of the disappearances. He denies there is a great mystery here. In the preface to his book *The Bermuda Triangle Mystery—Solved*, Kusche says, "Just a little imagination, a few silly unanswered questions . . . can turn almost anything into a mystery."

Maybe. Maybe not. So many questions remain. Where is the *Cyclops*? Why hasn't even a scrap of wreckage from Flight 19 been found? What happened to Carolyn Cascio and her passenger?

Adi-Kent Thomas Jeffrey, in her book *The Bermuda Triangle*, declares that "the Triangle Mystery is a challenge to us. Man is ever urging forward in trying to unravel the Unknown. And if there is something to be uncovered and discovered, he will find it out. He always has."

Until then, the mystery remains.

For Further Exploration

Books

Elwood D. Baumann, *The Devil's Triangle.* New York: Franklin Watts, 1976.

Charles Berlitz, *The Bermuda Triangle.* Garden City, NY: Doubleday, 1974.

————, *Without a Trace.* Garden City, NY: Doubleday, 1977.

Peter Briggs, *Men in the Sea.* New York: Simon & Schuster, 1968.

Daniel Cohen, *Monsters, Giants, and Little Men from Mars.* Garden City, NY: Doubleday, 1975.

————, *Mysterious Disappearances.* New York: Dodd, Mead, 1976.

Michael J. Cusack, *Is There a Bermuda Triangle?* New York: Julian/A Division of Simon & Schuster, 1976.

James M. Deem, *How to Catch a Flying Saucer.* Boston: Houghton Mifflin, 1991.

Edward F. Dolan Jr., *The Bermuda Triangle and Other Mysteries of Nature.* New York: Franklin Watts, 1980.

————, *Great Mysteries of the Sea.* New York: Dodd, Mead, 1984.

John Harris, *Without a Trace.* New York: Atheneum, 1981.

Adi-Kent Thomas Jeffrey, *The Bermuda Triangle*. New York: Warner, 1975.

George Johnson and Don Tanner, *The Bible and the Bermuda Triangle*. Plainfield, NJ: Logos International, 1973.

Lawrence Kusche, *The Bermuda Triangle Mystery—Solved*. Buffalo, NY: Prometheus, 1986.

————, *The Disappearance of Flight 19*. New York: Harper & Row, 1980.

Richard Michael Rasmussen, *Extraterrestrial Life*. San Diego, CA: Lucent Books, 1990.

Carl Sagan, *Intelligent Life in the Universe*. San Francisco: Harper, 1966.

Simon Seymour, *Strange Mysteries from Around the World*. New York: Four Winds Press, 1980.

Dale Titler, *Wings of Mystery*. New York: Dodd, Mead, 1966.

Alan Villiers, *Wild Ocean*. New York: Scribner's, 1974.

Harold T. Wilkins, *Strange Mysteries of Time and Space*. New York: Citadel, 1958.

Richard Winer, *The Devil's Triangle*. New York: Bantam, 1974.

Periodicals

Martin Caidin, "The Triangle with Four (or More) Sides," *Fate*, January 1993.

Michael J. Cusack, "The Deadly Mystery of the 'Devil's Triangle,'" *Science World*, September 20, 1973.

Clive Cussler, "Who's Afraid of the Bermuda Triangle?" *Ladies' Home Journal*, January 1978.

Geo, "Undersea Gas Leaks May Explain Bermuda Triangle Mystery," November 1982.

Bill Hewitt et al., "The Sea Yields Its Lost Squadron," *People*, June 3, 1991.

Jim Martenhoff, "The Devil's Triangle," *Boating*, November 1974.

John Miller, "Eyewitness in the Bermuda Triangle," *Fate*, January 1993.

Carleton Mitchell, "The Bermuda Triangle," *Boating*, October 1984.

Newsweek, "Bermuda Triangle, Facts and Fiction," July 18, 1983.

———, "Graveyard of the Atlantic," December 16, 1974.

Tom Post et al., "The Mystery of the Lost Patrol," *Newsweek*, May 27, 1991.

Scientific American, "The Mystery of the *Cyclops*," May 1934.

James Stewart-Gordon, "What's the Truth About the Bermuda Triangle?" *Reader's Digest*, July 1975.

Time, "A Deadly Triangle," January 6, 1975.

———, "It's Still the Lost Squadron," June 17, 1991.

———, "Lost Squadron," May 27, 1991.

Works Consulted

Books

Charles Berlitz, *Atlantis, the Eighth Continent*. New York: Putnam, 1984.

Robert F. Burgess, *Sinkings, Salvages, and Shipwrecks*. New York: American Heritage, 1970.

Charles J. Cazeau and Stuart D. Scott Jr., *Exploring the Unknown: Great Mysteries Reexamined*. New York: Plenum, 1979.

Lawrence Fawcett and Barry J. Greenwood, *The UFO Cover-Up*. Englewood Cliffs, NJ: Prentice Hall, 1984.

Carol A. Fuchs, *Disappearances*. Mankato, MN: Capstone Press, 1991.

Vincent H. Gaddis, *Invisible Horizons*. Philadelphia: Chilton, 1965.

John Godwin, *This Baffling World*. New York: Hart, 1968.

Francis Hitching, *The Mysterious World, An Atlas of the Unexplained*. New York: Holt, Rinehart & Winston, 1979.

Philip J. Klass, *UFOs: The Public Deceived*. Buffalo, NY: Prometheus, 1983.

Frank W. Lane, *Nature Parade*. New York: Sheridan House, 1954.

Patrick Moore, *Space Travel for the Beginner*. New York: Press Syndicate of the University of Cambridge, 1992.

Ivan T. Sanderson, *Invisible Residents*. New York: World, 1970.

Joshua Slocum, *Sailing Alone Around the World*. New York: Dover, 1956.

Gardner Soule, *Under the Sea*. New York: Meredith, 1968.

John Wallace Spencer, *Limbo of the Lost*. New York: Bantam, 1969.

———, *Limbo of the Lost—Today*. New York: Bantam, 1975.

———, *No Earthly Explanation*. New York: Bantam, 1975.

Periodicals

Associated Press, "Wind Shear Cited as Possible Factor in Shuttle Explosion," *Minneapolis Star and Tribune*, March 28, 1986.

Paul Chance, "Parapsychology Is an Idea Whose Time Has Come," *Psychology Today*, October 1973.

Literary Digest "Blaming the Giant Octopus for the 'Cyclops' Mystery," March 8, 1919.

———, "Disappearance of the 'Cyclops'—Another Mystery of the Deep," June 8, 1918.

Conrad A. Nervig, "The *Cyclops* Mystery," U.S. Naval Institute *Proceedings*, July 1969.

Janice Nurski, "Frozen Fuel," *Nature Canada,* Summer 1985.

Other

"The Bermuda Triangle and the Earth's Magnetism," Fact sheet, U.S. Department of Commerce, National Oceanic and Atmospheric Administration, April, 1986.

Fact sheet, 7th Coast Guard District, Miami, Florida, 1986.

Graham Massey, "The Case of the Bermuda Triangle," Vestron, Inc., Video for *NOVA*, BBC Enterprises, 1988.

Sea Quest, "Terror in the Bermuda Triangle," NBC-TV, November 7, 1993.

Index

Abacos Islands, 96

Apollo 12, 47

Atalanta, HMS,
   disappearance of, 27-30

Atlantic Ocean, 29, 39, 40, 43
   Carthaginian exploration of, 20
   Sargasso Sea as part of, 20-22

Atlantis, 82-84

Atlantis, the Eighth Continent (Berlitz),
   55

Avenger, TBM (WWII bomber), 13, 92,
   94

Azores, 28, 31

Bahama Islands, 16, 41
   strange occurrences near, 42, 47, 70,
      78, 82

Barbados, 27, 56

Bermuda, 16
   disappearances near
      HMS *Atalanta*, 27, 29-30
      Star Tiger, 38
   strange occurences near, 53, 86

Bermuda Triangle
   boating traffic in, 67-68
   compass irregularities and, 51-53
   described, 15-17
   eddies and, 42-43
   gas leaks and, 46-48

hurricanes and, 34

lack of wreckage in, 17, 70

magnetic fields and, 50-55, 81-82

naming of, 15

ocean currents and, 40

psychic experiences and, 79-81

science and, 17, 18, 32, 79-80

science fiction and, 76

sea monsters and, 75

time and, 76-84

UFOs and, 84-91

weather and, 38-40

winds and, 48-50, 78

see also Sargasso Sea

*Bermuda Triangle Mystery—Solved,
   The* (Kusche), 23, 26, 31, 38-39, 60,
   62, 75, 81

*Bermuda Triangle and Other Mysteries
   of Nature, The* (Dolan), 42

Bermuda Triangle, The (Berlitz), 12, 15,
   17, 18, 47, 78, 81

Bible and the Bermuda Triangle, The
   (Johnson and Tanner), 88-89

Birkemeier, William P., 50

Brown, Hugh Auchincloss, 55

Brown, Ray, 83-84

Bruun, Anton, 75

Caicos Trader (ship), 42-43

Caidin, Martin S., 53-54
Caribbean Sea, 16, 34, 40, 68
Cascio, Carolyn,
　disappearance of, 81-82, 97
caves, undersea, 70
Cayce, Edgar, 82-84
Challenger, space shuttle, 49-50
Columbus, Christopher
　glowing white streaks observed by, 47
　Sargasso Sea experiences of, 23
　maritime skills of, 35
compass irregularities, 51-53
Cousteau, Jacques, 70
crystals, underwater, 83-84
currents, sea, 40
　see also Gulf Stream
Cyclops, USS
　disappearance of, 56-62
　possible mutiny on, 65-66
　quicksand and, 70
　sea creatures and, 72-73, 75

Deep See (ship), 92, 94
Devil's Sea, 51
Devil's Triangle. *See* Bermuda Triangle
Devil's Triangle, The (Baumann), 85
Disappearance of Flight 19, The
　(Kushe), 95-96
doldrums, 40

eddies, 42-43
Einstein, Albert, 81
England, 27-28
Evans, John, 15
extrasensory perception, 79, 82

Fate magazine, 53, 70
fireballs. *See* lightning, ball
Flight 19
　attempted rescue of, 14-15, 61
　disappearance of, 10-14
　magnetic disturbances and, 55
　premonition about, 15
　search for wreckage of, 92-95
Florida, 16
　disappearances near, 39, 92
　strange occurrences near, 44, 55, 78,
　　86
Fort Lauderdale (Fla.) Naval Air
　Station, 10, 12, 55
Gaddis, Vincent H., 15
gas leaks, 46-47
Gernon, Bruce, 78
Good News (ship), 52-53
Great Mysteries of the Air (Barker), 84
Gulf of Mexico, 13, 34
Gulf Stream, 22, 29, 40-42, 43, 68

Havana, Cuba, 26
Henry, Don, 52-53, 55
hijacking, 66-68
Hill, Barney and Betty, 89-90
Himilco of Carthage, 20
Hispaniola, 35
horse latitudes, 24
hurricanes, 32-35

Intelligent Life in the Universe (Carl
　Sagan), 87
Invisible Horizons (Gaddis), 54-55
Invisible Residents (Sanderson), 25, 78
Is There a Bermuda Triangle? (Cusack),

23, 32, 40, 62
Isles of the Devils, 27

Japan, 51

Kosnar, Allan, 10, 15

lightning, ball, 35-37
Limbo of the Lost (Spencer), 30-31
Lindbergh, Charles, 51-52
Lost Squadron. *See* Flight 19

magnetic fields
  asteroids and, 55
  compass irregularities and, 51-53
  the earth and, 51
  extraterrestrial matter and, 84
  time eddies and, 81-82
  yellow hazes and, 53-54
  McIver, Richard, 46, 47
mutiny on the *Cyclops*, 65-66
*Mysterious World, An Atlas of the
  Unexplained, The* (Hitching), 35-36, 51

North Pole, 51
Nurski, Janice, 46-47

parallel universe, 81
People magazine, 13, 15, 92, 94
pilot error, 69-70
pirates, 62, 66
Plato, 82, 84
Poole, Don, 95
Project Bluebook, 91
Project Sign, 91
Puerto Rico, 16

pyramid, undersea, 18

Revonoc, the,
  disappearance of, 39
Rosalie, the
  disappearance of, 26
Royal Navy, (British), 27, 30

Sagan, Carl, 87
Sargasso Sea
  breeding of eels in, 75
  Columbus's reports of, 23
  deepwater eddies in, 43
  description of, 20-22, 25
  fear of, 31
  horse latitudes and, 24
sea monsters, 74-75
seamanship, lack of, 68-69
seiche waves, 45
Slater, Norman, 79
Slocum, Joshua,
  disappearance of, 62-65
Spray, (ship), 62-65
squid, giant, 72-74
Star Tiger, the,
  disappearance of, 38
Star Trek, 76
St. Elmo's fire, 37
St. Lawrence River, 53, 55
submarines, 58-59
Swallow, John, 43

Taylor, C.C., 12, 13, 95, 96
This Baffling World (Godwin), 85, 87
time eddies, 81-82
time warps, 76, 78

trade winds, 40
tsunami waves, 44-46
*Twenty Thousand Leagues Under the
    Sea* (Jules Verne), 76

UFOs (Unidentified Flying Objects),
    84-91
    the military and, 90-91
    underwater, 88-89
U.S. Coast Guard
    on causes of disappearances, 32,
        38-39, 68-69
    fact sheet on the Triangle, 17
    on hijacking, 67
    on unpredictable storms, 44-45

waterspouts, 43-44
West Indies, 27, 34, 69
whirlpools. *See* eddies
Wild Goose (fishing boat), 42
Wild Ocean (Villiers), 24-25
wind shear, 48-50
Without a Trace (Harris), 56
Woods Hole Oceanographic Institution,
    18, 43

yellow haze, 53-54

About the Author

Norma Gaffron, a former elementary school teacher, lives in New Brighton, Minnesota. She and her husband have three adult children. She has been writing professionally for the past fifteen years. Her articles, on topics as diverse as sailing, snakes, and replanting lost teeth, have appeared in many national magazines. She has been a Junior Great Books leader, and for six years she was a regional co-advisor for the Society of Children's Book Writers and Illustrators.

Gaffron and her family have sailed in the Bermuda Triangle several times and survived unscathed. Her interest in the stories about this area motivated her to write the first edition of this book. Since then she has written three other books in the Great Mysteries series: *Bigfoot*, *Unicorns*, and *El Dorado: Land of Gold*. Her book *Dealing with Death*, is part of the Overview Series for Lucent Books.

"One of the great things about writing nonfiction," says Gaffron, "is that you learn so much. When I uncover some information I've been searching for, I feel a real sense of triumph! Then to be able to share this information in the form of a book is extremely satisfying."

Picture Credits